Cambridge Elements ≡

Elements in the Philosophy of Physics
edited by
James Owen Weatherall
University of California, Irvine

IDEALIZATIONS
IN PHYSICS

Elay Shech
Auburn University

CAMBRIDGE
UNIVERSITY PRESS

Shaftesbury Road, Cambridge CB2 8EA, United Kingdom

One Liberty Plaza, 20th Floor, New York, NY 10006, USA

477 Williamstown Road, Port Melbourne, VIC 3207, Australia

314–321, 3rd Floor, Plot 3, Splendor Forum, Jasola District Centre, New Delhi – 110025, India

103 Penang Road, #05-06/07, Visioncrest Commercial, Singapore 238467

Cambridge University Press is part of Cambridge University Press & Assessment, a department of the University of Cambridge.

We share the University's mission to contribute to society through the pursuit of education, learning and research at the highest international levels of excellence.

www.cambridge.org
Information on this title: www.cambridge.org/9781108925044

DOI: 10.1017/9781108946742

First published 2023

A catalogue record for this publication is available from the British Library.

ISBN 978-1-108-92504-4 Paperback
ISSN 2632-413X (online)
ISSN 2632-4121 (print)

Idealizations in Physics

Elements in the Philosophy of Physics

DOI: 10.1017/9781108946742
First published online: January 2023

Elay Shech
Auburn University

Author for correspondence: Elay Shech, eshech@auburn.edu

Abstract: Idealizations are ubiquitous in physics. They are distortions or falsities that enter into theories, laws, models, and scientific representations. Various questions suggest themselves: What are idealizations? Why do we appeal to idealizations and how do we justify them? Are idealizations essential to physics and, if so, in what sense and for which purpose? How can idealizations provide genuine understanding? If our motivation for believing in the existence of unobservable entities like electrons and quarks is that they are indispensable to our best theories, should we also believe in the existence of indispensable idealizations? This Element will tackle such questions and offer an opinionated and selective introduction to philosophical issues concerning idealizations in physics. Topics to be covered include the concept of and reasons for introducing idealization, abstraction, and approximation, possible taxonomy and justification, and application to issues of mathematical Platonism, scientific realism, and scientific understanding.

This Element also has a video abstract: www.cambridge.org/Philosophy of Physics_ Elay Shech_abstract

Keywords: idealization, abstraction, approximation, scientific models, scientific representation

ISBNs: 9781108925044 (PB), 9781108946742 (OC)
ISSNs: 2632-413X (online), 2632-4121 (print)

Contents

1 Introduction

Milk production at a dairy farm was so low that the farmer wrote to the local university, asking for help from [scientists]. A multidisciplinary team of professors was assembled, headed by a theoretical physicist, and two weeks of intensive on-site investigation took place. The scholars then returned to the university, notebooks crammed with data, where the task of writing the report was left to the team leader. Shortly thereafter [the physicist returned to the farm in order to explain the report to the farmer. He asked for a blackboard and then drew a circle. He began:] "Assume the cow is a sphere . . . ."

(Harte 1988, xiii)

Idealizations are widespread and pervasive in physics. They are distortions or falsities that enter into theories, laws, models, or, more generally, scientific descriptions and representations. Examples include the frictionless plane, the simple pendulum, point and test particles, nonviscous fluid flow, infinitely thin wires and infinitely long cylinders or planes, a perfect vacuum, the ideal gas law, the Bohr model of the atom, the Ising and Hubbard models, and, of course, perfectly spherical cows.

Various questions suggest themselves: What are idealizations? Why do we appeal to idealizations and how do we justify them? Are idealizations essential to physics and, if so, in what sense and for which purpose? How can idealizations that are false and inaccurate afford true explanations, accurate descriptions, and genuine understanding? If our motivation for believing in the existence of unobservable entities like electrons and quarks is that they are indispensable to our best theories, should we also believe in the existence of indispensable idealizations? Would this mean that idealizations are abstract objects akin to Platonic forms, or fictions like literary characters? Instead, are essential idealizations paradoxical? Many other such questions arise.

The goal of this Element is to introduce the reader to philosophical issues concerning idealizations in physics and to provide a concise introduction to the relevant literature. In the sections that follow I will tackle some of the questions just raised. Unfortunately, due to limitations of space, my discussion will be far from comprehensive in either breath or depth, and hence many important contributions will be mentioned only in passing or else not at all. For example, although lots of the literature on idealization in physics concerns issues such as explanation (Batterman 2002; Batterman and Rice 2014; Bokulich 2008; Jansson Forthcoming), confirmation (Shaffer 2012, ch. 3), mathematical representation and applicability (Bueno and French 2018; Pincock 2012), reduction and emergence (Batterman 2002; Palacios 2022; Shech 2019a), and so forth, I will not have room to discuss these. The topic concerning how idealized claims or models, which are false or nonveridical, can provide scientific explanation will not be treated explicitly, for instance.[1] My approach then is to cover a limited number of topics by interacting critically with a small subset of recent contributions.[2]

What further complicates our study is that the notion of idealization is entangled with other issues that necessitate a detailed treatment (Fletcher et al. 2019a; Shech 2018a; Shech et al. 2022). For instance, some distinguish between idealization and abstraction (Jones 2005), and idealization and approximation (Norton 2012). Theories (French 2020), laws (Cartwright 1983; Liu 2004), models (Frigg and Hartmann 2020; Gelfert 2016; Jacquart Forthcoming), simulations (Humphreys 2004; Winsberg 2010), and representations (Frigg and Nguyen 2020; Shech 2015a, 2016) tend to be the objects that are idealized in some sense. Approximate truth (Oddie 2016) and analogy (Bartha 2019) are candidate relations that hold between what I call the "vehicle" of idealization and its "target" (Shech 2015a). Thought experiments (Stuart 2018) often involve a plethora of idealizations. The list goes on. Nevertheless, idealizations are interesting in their own right. Accordingly, insofar as possible, I concentrate specifically on *idealizations* in *physics*. For other reviews see Hüttemann (2002) for idealizations in physics, Elliott-Graves and Weisberg (2014) for idealizations more generally, and Shech and colleagues (2022) for connections with representation and explanation. For issues concerning infinite and infinitesimal idealizations see Shech (2018a) and the essays in Fletcher and colleagues (2019b).

The structure of the rest of the Element is as follows. Section 2 will discuss the concept of idealization and identify reasons requiring the introduction of idealization. I will distinguish between idealization broadly and narrowly construed and give two examples of the latter notion via a distinction between idealization and abstraction, and idealization and approximation. Section 3 will consider a well-received taxonomy of idealizations and Section 4 will discuss justificatory issues. Sections 5, 6, and 7 will connect between idealizations and the topics of mathematical Platonism, scientific realism, and scientific understanding. Section 8 ends the Element with a short summary. Last, in what remains of the Introduction I present two examples from physics that involve various idealizations.

Brownian motion concerns the jiggling seen under a microscope of particles like pollen suspended in a liquid. Taking a dilute solution of sugar (the solute) in

---

[1] See Rice (2021) for a recent discussion.
[2] My sincere apologies to all of the authors with important and insightful contributions to the debate that I have left out due to limitations of space.

water (the solvent) as his target system of interest and modeling said target as solid spheres suspended in a fluid solvent allowed Albert Einstein to infer the size of said molecules and Avogadro's constant (Einstein 1926/ 1956). While the phenomenon of Brownian motion is an actual effect found in the real world, the model of the water-sugar solution is highly idealized since it represents the sugar molecules as solid spheres and the water molecules as a fluid solvent in which the sugar molecules are suspended. Einstein also appealed to other idealizations such as abstracting away the inertia of the translation and rotational motions of the sugar molecules, assuming that any molecule's motion is unaffected by the motion of other molecules and that motion is only due to the stress at the surface, ignoring external forces such as gravity, and so on (Cheng 2013, 5). Additionally, he assumed that the equations of classical hydro-dynamics that pertain to fluids will be applicable to the molecular system, thereby idealizing away the complexities involved in the consideration of molecular structure (Einstein 1926/1956, 36–37). All such assumptions in the construction and application of the rigid-sphere model of the water-sugar solution are examples of idealizations, abstractions, and approximations (which I will discuss further in the following section).

The primary example I will refer to throughout the Element is the Aharonov–Bohm (AB) effect. Due to its somewhat technical nature, I will first present the case study qualitatively and only then add some technical details. To begin, recall that, when one shines a beam of homogenous light on a screen with two slits, an interference pattern with dark and light fringes emerges on a detector screen. It is possible to also produce interference patterns with particles like electrons (Figure 1, left), which arise from the buildup of single electrons (Figure 1, right).

Next consider how a beam of electrons would be affected by the introduction of a magnetic field, say, by adding a cylindrical solenoid and turning it "on." Due to the presence of charged particles moving through a magnetic field, the Lorentz force will act on the electrons as they navigate their way through the double-slit apparatus. Such an interaction can be understood in the context of classical physics, the consequence of which will be a shift in the interference pattern emerging on the detector screen (however, the presence of a wavelike interference pattern on the detector screen due to particle-like electrons would certainly be a surprise in a classical context).

Now contemplate what would happen if the recently introduced magnetic field was *completely* shielded from the electron beam. One can accomplish such a feat by making use of idealizations (I1–I3) (see Figure 2):

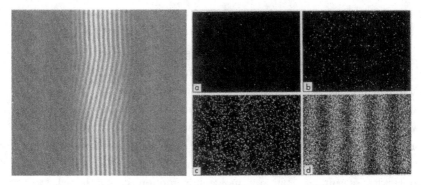

Figure 1 (Left) An example of an interference pattern from a double-slit experiment (from Möllenstedt and Bayh 1962, 304). (Right) Single-electron buildup of (biprism) interference pattern (from Tonomura 1999, 15). (a) 8 electrons, (b) 270 electrons, (c) 2,000 electrons, and (d) 60,000 electrons.

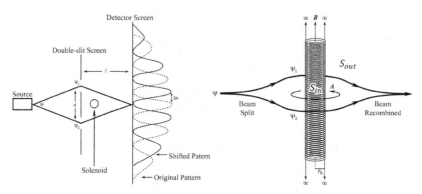

Figure 2 An illustration of the (magnetic) AB effect

I1. The cylindrical solenoid is assumed to be infinitely long so that no magnetic field spills outside of the solenoid once it is already "on."

I2. When the solenoid is turned "on" the magnetic field generated is completely contained within the solenoid so that no magnetic field spills outside of the solenoid as it is starting up.

I3. The solenoid is absolutely impenetrable so that the probability of finding an external electron in the region inside the solenoid is zero.

It is perhaps worthwhile to note that there is a plethora of other idealizations that are rarely explicitly mentioned. For instance, concentrating on I1, the infinite cylindrical solenoid is usually assumed to be made up of an infinitely thin wire that is wound infinitely tightly, and the current through the solenoid is assumed to be made up of uniformly circulating point charges. More generally, as Dougherty (2021, 12207) notes, the double-slit setup will be affected by various negligible factors such as "the Earth's electromagnetic field, the electron's emission and absorption of stray Z bosons, and the gravitational influence of Sagittarius A*." A full description of the apparatus "might involve an analysis of the interaction between the incident electron and the silver halide in the photographic plate, the subsequent emission of an electron from the silver halide and absorption by a nearby silver ion, the development and fixing of the image, and so forth" (15).

In any case, let us return to the issue at hand: What happens to the interference pattern in the double-slit experiment with electrons with a completely shielded magnetic field? Since there is no region in space in which the electron beam and magnetic field can causally interact, we would not expect any special effect to manifest according to classical physics.

In contrast, in their celebrated paper, Yakir Aharonov and David Bohm (1959) showed that nonrelativistic quantum mechanics (QM) predicts a shift in interference pattern in the aforementioned idealized scenario, and that such an effect can ostensibly be confirmed in the laboratory. Their paper became immensely influential (e.g., *Physical Review* counts 4,855 citations and Google Scholar counts 8,861), but it also sparked a heated 30-year controversy in the physics literature. Aharonov and Bohm (1959) and an alleged experimental confirmation of the AB effect by Chambers (1960) were met with particular skepticism and resistance.

At least four main issues were concurrently discussed: (1) One concerns whether the AB effect is a real and empirically verifiable effect that has been confirmed by laboratory experiments; another has to do with (2) what exactly the AB effect is in the first place. (3) An additional point of contention concerned the fundamental, ontological causal mechanism that brings about the AB effect – for example, is it due to the magnetic field/flux or the "electromagnetic vector potential" (which is generally regarded as mathematical fluff without physical significance)?[3] (4) Depending on one's take on (1)–(3), another issue has to do with the foundational implications (or lack thereof) of the AB effect. For instance, does the AB effect signify a novel kind of indeterminism or nonlocality (action at a distance)? In what follows, I describe the AB effect case study in detail and introduce several distinctions. The material is based on Shech (2018b, 2022a). I also follow Earman (2019) closely. The reader should feel free to skip or skim the details, returning to this section when necessary.

---

[3] In classical electromagnetism, electric and magnetic fields (and their respective fluxes) are considered to have genuine physical significance – they exist in the world. However, one can mathematically represent a magnetic field with an electromagnetic vector potential, but the relation is one to many: different potentials can represent the same magnetic field. Classically, we take this to mean that the potential has no physical significance – the many potentials corresponding to a particular field are just different ways of describing the same physical magnetic field. Roughly, foreshadowing discussion to come, choosing a particular potential corresponds to picking a "gauge" and any transformation of the potential that leaves the magnetic field invariant is a "gauge transformation" so that magnetic field is a "gauge-invariant" quantity.

A coherent beam of electrons (symbolized by ψ) is shot at a double-slit screen and split into two components (symbolized by ψ_1 and ψ_2), each passing on opposite sides of an infinite and impenetrable cylindrical solenoid S_∞ (where S_{in} represents the region inhabited by S_∞ and S_{out} the region outside of S_∞) and then made to recombine at the detector screen, where an interference pattern arises (see Figure 2). The solenoid is turned "on" and the interference pattern shifts by an amount $\Delta x = \dfrac{l\lambda e}{2\pi d\hbar}\Phi_\infty$, where λ is the wave length of the electron, e the charge of the electron, $\hbar$ the reduced Planck constant, d the distance between slits, l the distance between the double-slit screen and the detector screen, and Φ_∞ the magnetic flux through S_∞ when the solenoid is turned "on." The shift in pattern due to the shielded flux is what we call the AB effect narrowly construed or *narrow AB effect* for short (Earman 2019).[4]

The standard Hamiltonian operator for a charged *quantum* particle in a *classical* magnetic field takes the form of $H = \left(\boldsymbol{p} - \dfrac{e}{c}\boldsymbol{A}\right)^2$, where $\boldsymbol{A}$ is the electromagnetic vector potential operator (hereafter the potential), $\boldsymbol{p} = -i\nabla$ is the momentum operator, e and c are constants, and units have been chosen so that the mass of the electron is 1/2 and $\hbar = 1$. Such a setup gives rise to an additional idealization at the level of the governing theory. Namely, although a "true" or "realistic" description of the AB effect setup ought to appeal to relativistic field-theoretic quantum electrodynamics, our discussion arises in the "bastardized quantum-classical theory" that appeals to "an external unquantized electromagnetic field and an electron quantized in non-relativistic quantum mechanics" (Earman 2019, 2014–2016). In such a semiclassical setting, the idealizations I1–I3 give rise to the following differential operator: $H^{A_\infty} = \left(\boldsymbol{p} - \dfrac{e}{c}\boldsymbol{A}_\infty\right)^2$. In the Coulomb gauge of classical electromagnetism with polar coordinate (ρ, z, θ), $\rho := (x^2 + y^2)^{1/2}$, and with the z-axis chosen as the axis of S_∞ with radius R, the potential $\boldsymbol{A}_\infty$ takes the following form (so that the magnetic field in S_{out} is $\boldsymbol{B}_\infty = \nabla \times \boldsymbol{A}_\infty = 0$ as expected):

$$(A_\infty)_z = (A_\infty)_\rho = 0$$

$$(A_\infty)_\theta = \frac{\Phi_\infty}{2\pi\rho} \text{ for } \rho \geq R$$

$$(A_\infty)_\theta = \frac{\Phi_\infty\rho}{2\pi R^2} \text{ for } 0 \leq \rho \leq R$$

---

[4] This is the magnetic AB effect. There is an analog electric AB effect, implied by the Lorentz covariance, which arises from electric (instead of magnetic) fields, but I will concentrate on the magnetic AB effect in this Element (so by "AB effect" I mean the magnetic AB effect).

Given I1–I3, the configuration space for an electron is $\mathbb{R}^3 \backslash S_{in}$ (viz., $\mathbb{R}^3$ with S_{in} excised) since the probability of finding an electron in S_∞ is zero. This implies that H^{A_∞} is not "essentially self-adjoint" and thus neither determines the dynamics of the system nor is an "observable" in QM. In detail, the natural (initial) domain for H^{A_∞} is $D(H^{A_\infty}) = C_0^\infty(\mathbb{R}^3 \backslash S_{in})$, which is dense in $\mathcal{H} = L^2(\mathbb{R}^3 \backslash S_{in})$, where $C_0^\infty(\mathbb{R}^3 \backslash S_{in})$ are the smooth functions of compact support on $\mathbb{R}^3 \backslash S_{in}$, and $L^2(\mathbb{R}^3 \backslash S_{in})$ is the Hilbert space of complex valued square integrable functions on $\mathbb{R}^3 \backslash S_{in}$. Stone's theorem (Reed and Simon 1980, 266–268, Theorem VIII.8) implies that the dynamics of a quantum system are determined by a unitary group, where the infinitesimal generator of such a group must be a self-adjoint operator or an essentially self-adjoint operator such that there is a unique extension to a larger domain on which the operator is self-adjoint. H^{A_∞} is not essentially self-adjoint on its domain $D(H^{A_\infty})$, but it has an (infinity-fold) infinity of self-adjoint extensions with corresponding boundary conditions on the wave function at the border of the solenoid (de Oliveira and Pereira 2010).

The assumption I3 of impenetrability implies that the normal component j_N of the electron probability current j must vanish at the solenoid boundary (where $j := -i(\psi^* \nabla \psi - \psi \nabla \psi^*)$) (Earman 2019, 1999–2000). There are several sufficient (but not necessary) conditions for implementing this requirement using different boundary conditions including the Dirichlet boundary conditions ($\psi = 0$) that Aharonov and Bohm (1959) used, Neumann boundary conditions ($\nabla \psi = 0$), or Robin boundary conditions ($\nabla \psi = r\psi, r \in \mathbb{R}$) (de Oliveira and Pereira 2010, 7–8). Importantly, although any boundary condition can be used to derive the narrow AB effect (understood as a shift in interference pattern), different boundary conditions, which are related to different essentially self-adjoint extensions of H^{A_∞}, correspond to distinct dynamical evolutions with diverse empirical predictions for scattering experiments (see Figure 3). De Oliveira and Pereira (2010, 28) note that this confirms "the presence of the AB effect ... in different self-adjoint extensions," which (following Earman 2019) I refer to in the main text as the AB effect broadly construed or *broad AB effect* for short. *Key to the distinction* is that the choice of self-adjoint extension does not matter for the narrow AB effect but it does for the broad AB effect.

Aharonov and Bohm (1959) derived the narrow AB effect that concerns the shifted interference pattern in a double-slit experiment by making use of $\overline{H}_{AB}^{A_\infty}$, which is a self-adjoint extension of H^{A_∞} corresponding to Dirichlet boundary conditions. Specifically, they provided a semiclassical *approximation* of the relative phase shift picked up by the quantum state by assuming that the exact solution ψ_1 (of the Schrödinger equation with $\overline{H}_{AB}^{A_\infty}$) when the solenoid is turned

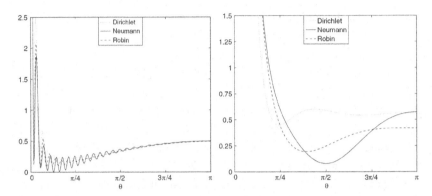

Figure 3 Predicted differential cross-section as a function of θ in the case of high energies (left) and in the case of intermediate energies (right), using Dirichlet, Neumann, and Robin boundary conditions. From de Oliveira and Pereira (2010, 25–27).

"on" is well approximated by the solution ψ_1' when the solenoid is turned "off" multiplied by a phase factor $e^{i\frac{e}{c}\Lambda_1}$, where $\Lambda_1 = \int_1 A \cdot dr$ is a scalar function corresponding to a line integral taken along a path in a (simply connected) region around the solenoid (and the same assumption is made for $\psi_2 = \psi_2' e^{i\frac{e}{c}\Lambda_2}$) (see Earman 2019, section 5.1, for details). This assumption is dubbed the Aharonov–Bohm (AB) *Ansatz* (Ballesteros and Weder 2009, 2011; Earman 2019), and it facilitates the prediction of a relative phase change $e^{i\theta} = e^{i\frac{e}{c}\Phi_\infty}$, where the shift in interference pattern depends on the magnetic flux Φ_∞. The AB *Ansatz* is another idealization of sorts. Consequently, Ballesteros and Weder (2009, 2011) showed that for high-velocity Gaussian electron wave packets the AB *Ansatz* is a good approximation for the type of systems used to confirm the AB effect experimentally, viz., with toroidal solenoids as in Tonomura and colleagues (1986).

Idealizations I1–I3 collectively ensure that the magnetic field and flux generated by the solenoid are *completely* shielded from the electron beam and vice versa. However, it is not possible to build an experimental setup of the sort since, for example, "infinitely repulsive barriers do not really exist" (Magni and Valz-Gris 1995, 179–180). Accordingly, I distinguish between the fictional, idealized, and theoretical effect, what I will call the *abstract AB effect*, which is the AB effect as it is conventionally defined, on one hand, and its physical counterpart, the *concrete AB effect* that has been allegedly confirmed in the laboratory since, arguably, experiments have come close enough to the ideal scenario. All together I have identified four "AB effects": abstract-narrow, abstract-broad, concrete-narrow, and concrete-broad (where the broad effects concern additional families of AB effects) (see Table 1). This ends my presentation of the AB effect case study. We will return to the role of idealizations in the AB effect throughout this Element but especially in discussing a taxonomy for idealizations (Section 3) and scientific understanding (Section 7). In the following section I discuss the concept of and the need for idealization more generally.

2 Idealization, Abstraction, and Approximation

What are idealizations and why do scientists use them in science? This section outlines possible answers found in the literature. It is worth noting at the start, however, that there is disagreement and inconsistency in the use of terms like "idealization" and "abstraction." My goal is to introduce the reader who may be unfamiliar with the literature to suggested characterizations before undertaking a more detailed discussion of particular characterizations.

Starting with the concept of idealization, Morrison (2015, 20), for instance, holds that idealization "involves a process of approximation whereby the system can" be represented to a greater degree of accuracy "by adding correction factors (such as friction to a model pendulum)." Potochnik (2017, 2) claims that idealizations "are assumptions made without regard for whether they are true, generally with the full knowledge that they are false." She stresses that an idealization is distinguished "in virtue of representing a system as if it were some way that it is not" (52) and that "little effort is put toward eliminating or even controlling" idealizations (42).

Reflecting on idealized models specifically, Frigg and Hartmann (2020) note that they "involve a deliberate simplification or distortion of something complicated with the objective of making it more tractable or understandable." For Pincock (2020, 4), an idealization is a false statement about a modeling target, which "is generated by the features of the model and the representational relation that it stands in to that target," such that "the agents using the model must believe that the statement is false." Shaffer (2012, 19–20) insists that idealizations must be accompanied by simplifications. Hüttemann (2002, 177–178) says that idealizations are "replacements of either mathematical descriptions, physical systems or data," which are "conscious and voluntary" and "more optimal" in some sense. This includes the production of physical systems, data interpolation, and data fitting (e.g., introducing error bars and

Table 1 Different types of the magnetic AB effect

	AB effects		
Abstract-narrow	**Abstract-broad**	**Concrete-narrow**	**Concrete-broad**
Interference shift derived by Aharonov and Bohm (1959) from $\overline{H}{}^{A_\infty}_{AB}$ (under idealizations I1–I3)	Any experimentally verifiable effects (such as scattering experiments) that depend on different self-adjoint extensions of H^{A_∞} (under idealizations I1–I3)	Physical manifestation of abstract-narrow effect (de-idealizing I1–I3)	Physical manifestation of abstract-concrete effect (de-idealizing I1–I3)

best-fit curves), as well as isolation, abstraction, neglect, and simplification. Nowak (2000) identifies five paradigms of idealizations in science:

- Neo-Duhemian paradigm: Idealization is a method of transforming raw data, such as when systematic errors are corrected, into data that can be used in the scientific enterprise.
- Neo-Weberian paradigm: Idealization is a method of constructing scientific notions.
- Neo-Leibnizian paradigm: Idealization is a deliberate falsification.
- Neo-Millian paradigm: Idealization is taken to be a consequence of the discrepancy between mathematical representation and the physical world.
- Neo-Hegelian paradigm: Idealization is a process that focuses only on essential and relevant features of some phenomenon.

And so on. Importantly, these characterizations are not equivalent. There is no agreement on whether idealization must include simplification, distortion, inaccuracy, misrepresentation, and/or failure of veridicality. Scholars discuss idealized models, simulations, representations, laws, theories, propositions, statements, systems, states of affairs, and worlds as possible vehicles (and sometimes targets) of idealization. Some consider the very act of representing parts of the world mathematically or even linguistically to involve an idealization of sorts.

It will thus be useful to distinguish between broad and narrow characterizations of idealizations. By *idealization broadly construed*, I intend anything at all (including the aforementioned characterizations) that could reasonably and intuitively be called an idealization, perhaps because a representational vehicle fails to meet some veridicality or accuracy condition. Reflecting on the Brownian motion example (Section 1), representing a water-sugar solution with a rigid-spheres-suspended-in-a-fluid model is an idealization, and so are Einstein's various nonveridical assumptions made for derivational purposes such as ignoring external forces or applying classical hydrodynamics. As for the AB effect case study (Section 1), examples of idealizations broadly construed include the entire semiclassical framework in which the AB effect is usually discussed, the whole of Aharonov and Bohm's (1959) double-slit gedankenexperiment, particularly claims I1–I3, the fictional or abstract system that contains S_∞, the various self-adjoint extensions of H^{A_∞}, the specific AB *Ansatz*, abstracting away from negligible factors such as stray electromagnetic and gravitational fields, and so on. I should emphasize that, unless noted otherwise, my use of the term "idealization" throughout this Element is to be understood as "idealizations broadly construed."

In contrast, *idealization narrowly construed* refers to various specific characterizations (like the ones presented earlier) that are offered by particular philosophers with certain aims in mind and that may thus be distinguished from similar notions such as abstraction, approximation, fiction, metaphor, and thought experiment. As an example, let us consider the notions of approximation and abstraction (which I will refer to in Sections 5 and 6).

John Norton (2012, 209) suggests that we distinguish between an "approximation" and an "idealization" as follows:

> An approximation is an inexact description of a target system. It is propositional. An idealization is a real or fictitious system, distinct from the target system, some of whose properties provide an inexact description of some aspects of the target system.

For instance, consider a body of unit mass falling in a weakly resisting medium. For gravitational constant g and friction coefficient k, its speed v at time t is given by: $\dfrac{dv}{dt} = g - kv$. Falling from rest, its speed as a function of time is given by the Taylor expansion series:

$$v(t) = \frac{g}{k}\left(1 - e^{-kt}\right) = gt - \frac{gkt^2}{2} + \frac{gk^2t^3}{6} - \cdots$$

The first term in the series expansion, $v(t) = gt$, is a good *approximation* (viz., an inexact description) of the fall for small k and at early times. $v(t) = gt$ is also the *exact* velocity of a fictitious idealized system with the same mass falling under gravity in a vacuum.

The idea then is that, if a property like $v(t) = gt$ is only used to inexactly describe a target system, then it is an "approximation." But if reference is made to a "real or fictitious system" with the exact property $v(t) = gt$, then said system is an "idealization." Our freedom to invoke either an approximation or an idealization means that we can "demote" an idealization to an approximation by choosing to describe a target system inexactly through the properties of an idealization, such as when we approximate the Taylor expansion with $v(t) = gt$. Similarly, it is sometimes possible to "promote" an approximation to an idealization by identifying and referring to the real or fictitious system that actually has the properties (like $v(t) = gt$) used to inexactly describe some target system.

Norton (2012, 211) explains that "An idealization can be demoted to an approximation by discarding the idealizing system and merely extracting the inexact description; however, the inverse promotion to an idealizing system will not always succeed." He therefore suggests that we dispense with idealization since "the approximation already tells us what we could learn from the idealization about the target system" (226). His worry is that, if we appeal to an idealization, then we risk attributing properties (of the idealized system) to the target system that it does not bear. However, at least two concerns come to mind with Norton's suggestion. First, to say that some proposition p is an inexact description of a target system (and thus a Nortonian approximation) is to say that p is approximately true or *truthlike*. But there are problems with various accounts of truthlikeness (Oddie 2016). Moreover, some approaches seem to make indispensable use of what is naturally characterized as a Nortonian idealization. For instance, Hilpinen's (1976) theory of approximate truth roughly says a proposition p is approximately true if and only if *there is a possible world in which p is true*, but such a possible world satisfies Norton's characterization of idealization. It is then odd to suggest that we dispense with idealizations when the very notion of an approximation is fleshed out by appeals to idealizations.

Second, as I explain in what follows (and in Section 4), what is considered an idealization will depend on one's theoretical background and historical period. Moreover, as Ruetsche (2011, 337) notes, theoretical "features made available by idealizations are likely to persist in future theories when those features function as guides for theory development" (337). This means that today's idealizations can both guide future theory and model construction, and be part of the nonidealized content of tomorrow's theory. For example, the emergence of novel theoretical features made available by idealization is exemplified in the AB effect with the many self-adjoint extensions of H^{A_∞}, which correspond to many different AB effects. Such novel theoretical features may endure in and thus guide the development of future theory, for example, in a field-theoretic analysis of the AB effect. In any case, insofar as idealizations in the AB effect (instead of Nortonian approximations) illuminate the foundations of quantum theory (Section 7, Earman 2019; Shech 2018b, 2022a), this suggests that it may be worthwhile to appeal to idealizations over approximations.

Before continuing, note that (although it isn't an explicit part of Norton's characterization) often the notion of approximation is used when it is clear how close we are to the sought-after solution. The example of the Taylor expansion shows that we can, in principle, get as close as we want to the exact solution $v(t) = \frac{g}{k}\left(1 - e^{-kt}\right)$ by including more and more terms from the expansion:

$$gt - \frac{gkt^2}{2} + \frac{gk^2t^3}{6} - \cdots.$$

Another distinction that is often made concerns the notion of abstraction that has been emphasized by Cartwright (1983) and also identified as "negligibility assumptions" (Musgrave 1981), the "method of isolation" (Mäki 1994), and "Aristotelian Idealization" (Frigg and Hartmann 2020). The basic idea is that, whereas idealizations are in some sense "literally false" or else they distort or misrepresent some aspect of a target, abstractions concern incomplete or partial truth. For instance, Godfrey-Smith (2009, 48) says:

> An abstract description of a system leaves a lot out. But it is not intended to say things that are literally false. An idealized description of a system is a description that fictionalizes in the service of simplification . . . The idealized description is often presented verbally as a description of a real system, but not a description that is literally true.

Similarly, Jones holds that "abstractions involve omission *without* misrepresentation" (2005, 175; original emphasis). Others characterize abstraction modally such that "abstraction is a process whereby we describe phenomena in ways that cannot possibly be realized in the physical world (for example, infinite populations)" (Morrison 2015, 20).

It is worthwhile to note that some emphasize the importance of distinguishing between the *process* of idealization/abstraction and the idealized/abstracted *product* of such a process. For instance, Levy (2018, 4) distinguishes between abstraction as a process of representational omission, that is, "moving to a detail-poor representation," and "abstractness," which designates the level of representational detail. While Jones and (to some extent) Godfrey-Smith hold that a representation cannot contain both idealization (misrepresentation/ falsity) and abstraction (incomplete representation/partial truth), Levy (2018) motivates the idea that representations can be idealized (inaccurate/false) but differ in level of abstractness so that the two notions are complementary. For example, while the statements "the speed of light in a vacuum is constant" and "the speed of light in a vacuum is c = 299,792,458 m/s" are true and so unidealized, the former is more abstract than the latter. Similarly, the statement "the speed of light in a vacuum is several hundred meters per second" and the more detailed statement "the speed of light in a vacuum is 300 m/s" are false and so idealized, but the former is more abstract than the latter. He thus suggests that "abstractness is not about fidelity to reality, but about *relative informativeness*" (4–5; original emphasis).

Likewise, Portides (2018) argues that we shouldn't ground the distinction between idealization and abstraction in terms of the distinct semantic properties (viz., false versus partially true) of their products but by the cognitive process involved. Namely, abstraction concerns selective attention to a subset of the *actual* total features of a target as if other features were absent. Idealization involves selective attention to a subset of all logically *possible* ways by which features of actual systems could be modified, as long as such modifications don't clash with received theoretical principles. He presents an example (19):

> [An] inertial reference frame . . . is a way to treat classical systems because it does not conflict with Classical Mechanics; in fact, Newton's first law of motion requires inertial reference frames. However, from the perspective of the Theory of General Relativity the classical notion of [an] inertial reference frame cannot exist globally, because according to theory free motion is motion on a geodesic and motion on a geodesic is motion in curved spacetime and such motion is accelerated motion. Thus treating a General Relativistic system as a classical inertial reference frame is not an idealization because it would conflict with theoretical principles.

The idea then is that treating noninertial frames as inertial is an idealization *relative to* Newtonian physics but not in relativistic physics.

To my mind, perhaps because inertial frames ostensibly clash with relativistic principles (in the aforementioned sense), we may want to call such systems idealizations. In any case, I think Portides's (2018) discussion brings to light two important related aspects of idealization. The first is that, generally, whether a representation is an idealization depends on how we take the world to actually be and that in turn depends on the background theory with which we are working. For example, in discussing appeals to infinite limits in the context of spontaneous symmetry breaking in quantum field theory (QFT), Earman (2004) notes that, while infinite limits may generally be construed as idealizations, there is a sense in which they are realistic descriptions in QFT where "matter is nothing but excitations in quantum fields":

> For example, even the humblest of vacuum states, the Minkowski vacuum, entails correlations between spacetime regions having an arbitrarily large spatial separation. Thus, intuitions retrained to fit QFT would think of all physical systems as being infinitely large while recognizing that for practical purposes some systems can be treated as spatially finite objects. (192)

Other examples include conceiving of light as a wave versus a ray relative to the wave and ray theories of light, respectively (Batterman 2002); representing matter as a continuum relative to classical thermodynamics and hydrodynamics instead of a classical particle relative to classical statistical mechanics (Darrigol 2013). Even in classical mechanics one may describe the fundamental objects as point masses relative to point-mass mechanics, rigid bodies relative to analytic mechanics, or flexible bodies relative to continuum mechanics (Wilson 2013) – all of which would be considered idealizations relative to QM or QFT.

Second, idealizations typically involve modal notions. Particularly if an idealized representation doesn't contradict the laws and principles of a theory, it will count as a possible system, phenomenon, or world according to said theory. For instance, infinitely long and absolutely impenetrable solenoids may be non-actual – in fact, perhaps given certain contingent facts about our world (e.g., finite resources), they may also be "non-actualizeable" in the sense that they are not practically possible – but they are not impossible. Such idealized objects don't contradict the laws and principles of semiclassical mechanics.

Similarly, while a truly frictionless plane may be practically impossible to build, it is nomologically possible with respect to classical physics (since frictionless objects don't contradict Newton's laws). Also, we are only likely to identify a system as idealized if it is different enough from some target in the world – that is, if it is some *possible* but non-actual system. What is possible will depend on the various notions of modality that one may be working with (e.g., logical, metaphysical, nomological, physical, chemical, biological) and on the background scientific theories to which one is committed.

Related, it isn't clear what distinguishes legitimate idealizations, abstractions, and approximations from downright impossibilities. For example, Ladyman (2008, 360–361) notes that idealized perfectly reversible engines ("Carnot engines"), which could never be built in practice, are part and parcel of the theory of thermodynamics, while a perpetual motion machine is absolutely barred by the same theory. But why are perfectly reversible engines idealizations, while perpetual motion machines are impossibilities? One potential answer is that the former arises as a structure that is asymptotically approached in some idealizing limit, while the latter cannot be reached via such a limiting procedure. This suggestion is controversial, however, and requires further study (Norton 2016; Palacios and Valente 2021; Valente 2019). After all, if by a thermodynamic reversible process we mean a system that is always in equilibrium and also isn't, then such systems are logically contradictory and thus impossible in a strong sense.

In addition, Psillos (2011) argues that focusing on the idealization/abstraction process motivates viewing the product as a fictitious entity, which he takes to be in tension with scientific realism. But if one concentrates on the theoretical description of the product itself, this suggests that the product of idealization/abstraction is an abstract entity. Moreover, he holds that the latter option is consistent with scientific realism. His analysis prompts a more general inquiry: What are idealizations ontologically speaking? Are they abstract entities or fictions (see Section 5)? Are they impossible objects (Levy 2015; Shech 2016; Toon 2012)? Do they concern propositions that can be true/false or non-semantic representations that may only be accurate/inaccurate?

Perhaps it is possible to appeal to division of labor in this context as the ontology of idealization/abstraction is likely parasitic on the ontology of those vehicles that are idealized/abstracted. So, for instance, if theories are vehicles of idealization, then idealizations will be ontologically whatever we take theories to be. French (2020) considers various views such as theories as sets of propositions, as families of models, as representations, as abstract entities, as abstract artifacts, and as fictions, and ultimately settles on an eliminativist position. A similar analysis of the ontology of idealizations can be conducted for laws, models, simulations, descriptions, and so forth.

For example, Shaffer (2012) appeals to the model-theoretic account of truth and argues that we should conceive of theoretical descriptions as representing idealized possible worlds that are incomplete, and that incomplete worlds ought to be identified with partial models that are further fleshed out via the notion of an "intensional relational structure" (Swoyer 1991). Details aside, he further argues that his account of models/worlds is compatible with various ontological views including Lewisian realism, moderate realism, conceptualism, fictionalism, and agnosticism (Shaffer 2012, 185–187).

Let us move on to our second main question of this section: why do scientists use idealizations in science? What are our *reasons* for introducing idealizations? There seem to be three main interdependent sources giving rise to the need for idealization. These include the world, science, and scientists. The basic idea is that the world and its phenomena are immensely rich and complex, human scientists are cognitively limited beings with various goals and changing interests, and science itself represents its objects incompletely. I will discuss each of these in turn, starting with the world.

In his review of effective field theory (EFT), Georgi (1993, 210) describes the situation aptly:

> One of the most astonishing things about the world in which we live is that there seems to be interesting physics at all scales. Whenever we look in a previously unexplored regime of distance, time, or energy, we find new physical phenomena. From the age of [the] universe, about 10^{18} sec, to the lifetime of a W or Z [boson], a few times 10^{-25} sec, in almost every regime we can identify physical phenomena worthy of study.

In other words, pick any spatiotemporal region of the universe at a particular scale, and you will find a plethora of interesting patterns and regularities to study. Potochnik (2017, 14) describes the situation similarly in identifying the ways the world is complex:

> First, there is simply a large variety of different phenomena . . . Second, there is an extensive range of influences on any phenomenon . . . Those influences are also phenomena in their own right, and they too vary immensely. Third, the influences on similar phenomena vary and also combine in different ways . . . Finally, there is even complexity in how individual influences affect phenomenon.

On her view, the world contains phenomena that "embody many patterns, perhaps *infinitely* many" (42; my emphasis) and it is such patterns or regularities that are the targets of scientific investigation.

Human scientists, though, are cognitively limited. Moreover, when studying phenomena scientists have many diverse goals, including representation, generality, explanation, understanding, manipulability, prediction, exploration, theory and model construction, and so forth, or their interests may be pedagogical or heuristic in nature. Idealization and abstraction, therefore, allow scientists to focus on patterns that are both amenable to scientific investigation in the sense that they are not overly complicated and relevant for the goal at hand. Georgi (1993, 210–211; original emphasis) explains:

> To do physics amid . . . remarkable richness [and complexity], it is convenient to be able to isolate a set of phenomena from all the rest, so that we can describe it without having to understand everything. Fortunately, this is often possible. We can divide the parameter space of the world into different regions, in each of which there is a different appropriate description of the important physics . . . The two key words here are *appropriate* and *important*. The word *important* is key because the physical processes that are relevant differ from one place in parameter space to another. The word *appropriate* is key because there is no single description of physics that is useful everywhere in parameter space . . . This is an old trick, without which much of our current understanding of physics would have been impossible.

The idea that "no single description of physics" is "useful everywhere" is reminiscent of Potochnik's (2017, 36) point, spoken more forcefully, that depicting "the full gamut of causal influences in a single representation is impossible." Certainly, if every phenomenon of interest embodies an infinite number of possible patterns of scientific study, then cognitively limited scientists will need to appeal to idealization/abstraction in order to focus on some finite subset of patterns. Also suggested here is that something about the nature of our best science itself, including the mathematical methods used, either introduces a need for idealization or makes it that idealizations are extremely useful. Let us consider some ways in which this may be the case.

First, on a very general level, whether we are considering theories, laws, models, and so forth, whether we describe the world scientifically via language or mathematics, science is a representational enterprise. But representation by its very nature is partial in at least two senses. For one, the only completely comprehensive and accurate representation of a target, in the strongest sense, is a perfect copy of the target itself. So any representation will be partial in the sense of being incomplete (or a imperfect copy). For another, by its very nature, to represent a target is to appeal to some *other* object that stands in for the target as the vehicle of representation. In this sense, representation always concerns idealization due to a discrepancy between the vehicle and the target, and can arise in the very act of describing observations and measurement with data tables and graphs, error bars, best-fit curves, and so forth.

Still, neither incompleteness nor a discrepancy between vehicle and target implies that a theory, law, or model can't realistically and accurately represent aspects of the world within its domain. However, often we appeal to conflicting representational vehicles in studying a regularity of interest, such as when we model the AB effect using both QM and classical electrodynamics.[5] Generally, given that different factors – gravitational, mechanical, electromagnetic, chemical, and so forth – can all act on a target system of interest, and given that a phenomenon may require simultaneously modeling a system at different scales, and, furthermore, given that many systems portray nonlinear behavior and are highly correlated, it is not always possible to neatly separate targets into nonoverlapping domains without additional appeals to idealization. Moreover, idealizations themselves facilitate combining representational vehicles such as when we invoke limiting relations between theories (Batterman 2002) or when they serve as "handshakes" between models from different theoretical frameworks (Winsberg 2010).

Second, in order to study particular patterns embodied in worldly phenomena, scientists appeal to idealizations in the sense that they treat systems as if they are isolated. Systems, though, are not isolated. Some interference is unavoidable, for example, gravitational interference cannot be "screened out." Nevertheless, systems are taken to be effectively isolated because scientists believe such outside interference is "controllable" in the sense that our best theories tell us either that said interference is negligible or that the effects introduced by interference can be "subtracted off" (Sklar 2000, 44). However, due to resonance, even a small and seemingly negligible force can have a substantial effect on a system if delivered with the right kind of periodicity (Sklar 2000, 52). Furthermore, there are various contexts in which the non-isolability of systems concerns important foundational issues and hence it isn't clear that the associated idealization of treating systems as if they are isolated is controllable. For example, in discussing relational versus substantialist concepts of space and mechanics, Sklar (2000, 46–47) notes:

> For Machians it is the "fixed starts," or, better, the averaged smeared-out mass of the universe, that provides the reference frame relative to which uniform motion is absolute uniform motion [instead of Newton's conception of absolute space] ... From the Machian perspective, then, the idealization of the

---

[5] Also see discussion of multiple-model idealization in Section 3.

systems treated in standard Newtonian theory as isolated is not merely the source of some kind of controllable error that we could put to the side by adding a *ceteris paribus* clause to our account of the systems' behavior. It is, rather, a fundamental conceptual error in the theory ... that leads to a total misunderstanding of the most fundamental aspects of dynamics.

Similarly, while the second law of thermodynamics is characterized for isolated systems – entropy never decreases for a closed system – approaches such as Ridderbos and Redhead's (1998) explain entropic behavior in terms of the non-isolability of systems: "Perturbations from outside serve as a kind of 'stirring mechanism' or 'source of randomness' that drives" systems to equilibrium (Frigg 2008, 164). Additionally, non-isolability plays important roles in interpretations of QM such as Bohm's hidden variable interpretation and the decoherent histories approach (Bacciagaluppi 2020). All these are examples of how the idealization of isolation may be uncontrollable and may concern important foundational issues.

Third, as noted, the world is complex. Complexity can arise due to various features associated with systems such as numerosity, disorder and diversity, feedback and resonance, nonequilibrium behavior, spontaneous order and self-organization, nonlinearity, robustness, nested structure and modularity, and so forth (Ladyman and Wiesner 2020). But even apparently simple systems are sometimes described by our best scientific theories in ways that are mathematically intractable and thus resist scientific analysis without appeals to idealizations. Following Goldstein and colleagues (2002, 121), one famous example is the Newtonian three-body problem, in which three bodies m_1, m_2, and m_3, at respective positions r_1, r_2, and r_3, interact via Newton's inverse square law of universal gravitation. Expressed in the center of mass system, the equations of motion of the first mass can be written simply (with analogous equations for the other two masses):

$$\ddot{r}_1 = -Gm_2 \frac{r_1 - r_2}{|r_1 - r_2|^3} - Gm_3 \frac{r_1 - r_3}{|r_1 - r_3|^3}$$

We can rewrite all three-equations in symmetrical form by introducing the relative-position vectors $s_j = r_i - r_k$ so that:

$$\ddot{s}_j = -mG \frac{s_j}{s_j^3} + m_j G, \tag{2.1}$$

where $j = 1, 2, 3$, $m = m_1 + m_2 + m_3$, and $G = G\left(\sum_j \frac{s_j}{s_j^3}\right)$. At this point, it is usually noted that the three coupled equations in Equation (2.1) "cannot be solved in general" (Goldstein et al. 2002, 122), "cannot be solved exactly" (Ladyman 2008, 258), or that "analytical solutions are not available" (Valtonen and Karttunun 2005, 221). It is perhaps worthwhile to note what such authors may intend by these claims. From a mathematical point of view, differential equations possibly have no solution or there may be many, that is, a solution may not be unique and the system described by such an equation would be indeterministic (e.g., see Norton's "Dome" in Norton (2008)). For a differential equation like 2.1, there are existence theorems (due to Picard, Lipschitz, and Cauchy) that guarantee the existence of a unique solution.[6]

What is typically meant then by said claims is that there are no known solutions to the *general* three-body problem expressed in terms of well-known functions such as polynomial, trigonometric, exponentials, and so forth, known as "closed-form solutions."[7] In contrast, for the two-body problem there are solutions that involve elliptic, parabolic, and hyperbolic orbits. That said, when applying Equation (2.1) to specific situations such as a sun–planet–asteroid system, significant simplifications can be made since the asteroid's gravitational attraction is negligible. In such cases we consider a *restricted* three-body problem and solutions have been found for particular situations – for example, by Leonhard Euler and Joseph-Louis Lagrange (see Figure 4).

That there are no "closed-form solutions" does not imply that there are no "analytic solutions" and, in fact, Karl Sundman (1912) found a general solution

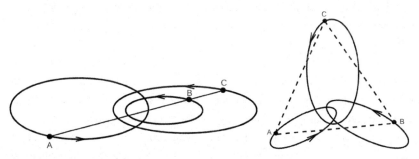

Figure 4 (Left) Euler's solution with a line joining three masses m_1, m_2, and m_3 located at the corresponding points A, B, and C. (Right) Lagrange's solution with an equilateral triangle joining m_1, m_2, and m_3 located at the corresponding points A, B, and C (from Musielak and Quarles 2014, 7).

---

[6] In slightly more detail, for an ordinary differential equation $\frac{dy}{dx} = f(y(x),(x))$ with initial condition $y(x_0) = y_0$ and x_0 being the initial value of $x \epsilon [x_0 - \varepsilon, x_0 + \varepsilon]$, if $f(y(x),(x))$ is a Lipschitz continuous function in y and x, then there is an $\varepsilon > 0$ such that a *unique* solution $y(x)$ *exists* on the interval $[x_0 - \varepsilon, x_0 + \varepsilon]$ (Musielak and Quarles 2014, 5–6).

[7] See Borwein and Crandall (2013) for varying characterizations of "closed-form solutions."

in terms of an (infinite) power series expansion (for most initial conditions).[8] Sundman's work was generalized by Quidong Wang (1991) as a solution to the more general n-body problem (omitting solutions leading to collisions). Interestingly, though, both solutions are unhelpful from the practical perspective of predicting three-body (or n-body) motions. The reason is these infinite series solutions converge very slowly: "One would have to sum up millions of terms to determine the motion of the particles for insignificantly short intervals of time" (Diacu 1996, 70).

While many solutions are inexact in the sense that they necessitate numerical methods and are thus only approximations, the round-off errors associated with the Sundman–Wang solutions make such series impracticable for numerical work. In fact, one source for the complexity associated with the three-body problem is its chaotic nature wherein a small perturbation to initial conditions can lead to radically divergent outcomes. This means that appeals to numerical methods and approximations will also be limited in their efficacy and, in any case, solutions obtained via such methods will be "inexact." It may also be the case that the chaotic nature of the system limits our ability to give exact results as contrasted with probabilistic ones. For instance (by making use of an ergodic hypothesis), Stone and Leigh (2019) report a formula that gives the probability distribution (instead of an exact description) of final states of the system given its initial state. This is another sense in which our best scientific and mathematical theories may represent aspects of the world (such as chaotic systems) in an approximated and idealized manner.

To conclude, below is an open-ended list, in the form of a table inspired by Potochnik (2017, 48), of the many reasons scientists appeal to idealizations (where it is admittedly ambiguous whether some reasons, such as complexity and non-isolability, are primarily due to the world or due to our best science and mathematics, given that the latter are our source for knowing about the former) (Table 2). Last, unless explicitly noted, recall that my use of the term "idealization" throughout the rest of this text is to be understood as idealizations broadly construed.

3 Taxonomy

There are various taxonomies of idealizations (e.g., McMullin 1985; Nowak 2000; Shaffer 2012). In this section, I present Weisberg's (2013) well-received taxonomy and critically evaluate it.

Weisberg (2013, ch. 6) holds that the activities and justification associated with idealization give rise to three kinds of idealizations: *Galilean idealizations*,

---

[8] For example, for Humphreys (2004, 62), "analytical solutions" are exact solutions expressed with closed forms or infinite series. See Ardourel and Jebeile (2017) for an interesting discussion.

Table 2 Reasons for appealing to idealizations, abstractions, and approximations

Due primarily to the world	Due primarily to scientists	Due primarily to science, math, and technology
• Myriad of phenomena at different scales • Complex nature of phenomena, e.g., numerosity, nonlinearity, chaos, resonance . . . • Non-isolability of systems	• Diverse research focus and goals • Pedagogical, heuristic, and/or pragmatic value • Cognitive limits • Simplification, ease of calculation • Highlighting irrelevancies, emphasizing salient difference-making factors	• Partial, incomplete nature of representation • Data fitting and interpolation • Limiting relations between theories • "Handshakes" between models • Computational limits • Mathematical intractability

• Facilitating scientific goals such as representation, generality, explanation, understanding, manipulability, empirical adequacy, (novel) prediction, exploration, theory and model construction.

minimalist idealizations, and *multiple-model idealizations* (where such notions are additional examples of idealizations narrowly construed from Section 2). Briefly, Galilean idealizations simplify and render computationally tractable the treatment of a target system. Minimalist idealizations expose the key factors that make a difference to the occurrence and character of a phenomenon of interest. Multiple-model idealizations are related but possibly incompatible models with different epistemic or pragmatic goals such as affording representations that are predictively precise, accurate or realistic, general in scope, simple, and so forth. We'll discuss each in turn but first note that Weisberg's taxonomy is structured by what he calls *representational ideals*, including *completeness, simplicity, 1-causal, maxout, a-general*, and *p-general* (all explained in what follows), which characterize the goals and standards used to construct and evaluate theoretical representations and models (Figure 5).

"Galilean idealization is the practice of introducing distortions into models with the goal of simplifying, in order to make them more mathematically or computationally tractable" (Weisberg 2013, 99). This suggests that the goal and thus the reason for introducing a Galilean idealization concerns computational

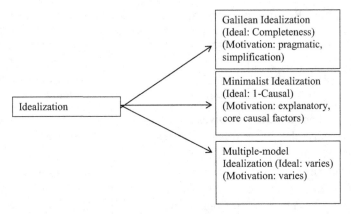

Figure 5 Weisberg's taxonomy of idealizations, where a multiple-model idealization can also include a Galilean or minimalist idealization as one of multiple models

tractability, for example, in order to make a prediction, and hence such idealization is justified pragmatically. In turn, advances in computational power and mathematical techniques should allow for de-idealization and ostensibly better prediction, so we expect such idealization to abate with scientific progress. For example, in Section 1 we saw that the AB effect shift in interreference pattern is derived with the aid of the AB *Ansatz*, which was later shown to be a good approximation for high-velocity Gaussian electron wave packets (Ballesteros and Weder 2009, 2011).

However, if we can use a model to make a prediction to some needed level of precision, why ought we to further de-idealize the model? Perhaps the representational ideal governing Galilean idealization is *maxout*, which states that precision and accuracy of model *output* ought to be maximized. De-idealization then is continually motivated by further maximizing predictive accuracy, but (as Weisberg notes) it may be the case that maximum predictive accuracy for some target of interest is in fact afforded by black-box models (say, of the kind we find in machine-learning contexts), in which case de-idealization would not be motivated. Instead, Weisberg explains that the representational ideal of Galilean idealization is *completeness*, where the ideal states that the best representation is one that represents – with the highest degree of precision and accuracy – all properties of the target phenomenon, all structural and causal relations, and any external aspects related to the target.

This clarifies why we ought to always expect Galilean idealization to be de-idealized. Still, while completeness motivates continual de-idealization, such an ideal seems tangential to mathematical tractability. For instance, simplifying idealizations in the AB effect, such as ignoring stray gravitational and electro-magnetic fields, impedes giving a complete representation. Thus, there seems to be a tension between the idea that Galilean idealization are introduced primarily for reasons of tractability and the ideal of completeness where one always expects such idealization to be de-idealized.

One may worry that I have overcomplicated the issue here. What Weisberg is suggesting is that idealization is "justified" by its predictive fruits, but the idealization is legitimized by the fact that it can, in principle, be de-idealized. In reply, first, I agree that this is Weisberg's general suggestion but I have argued that once Weisberg further identifies *completeness* as the ideal of Galilean idealization, a tension arises between the ideal and the motivation for introducing the idealizations. Second, our motivations for introducing idealizations given our goals and the various constraints placed on us by the world's complexity – *reasons* identified in Section 2 (see Table 2) – are markedly different from the epistemic and logical *justificatory* debt placed on us by our appeal to idealization. Such epistemic-justificatory debt needs to be discharged in the way of giving a justification for an idealization, that is, showing that the idealization is legitimized and explaining why it works. It is worthwhile to keep these two notions separated: there are reasons for introducing idealizations, including our motivations and goals, and there is the justification given. I will elaborate on the notion of and need for justification in Section 4.

Minimalist idealization, also known as *minimal models*, is governed by the representational ideal *1-causal*, which states that a theorist ought to only include "those factors that make a difference to the occurrence and essential character of the phenomenon in question" (Weisberg 2013, 100). The goal is primarily to provide scientific explanations and, insofar as only key difference-making factors are involved, there is no expectation that such idealization abates with scientific progress via de-idealization. For instance, Strevens's (2008) notion of minimalist idealization/model (which he calls a canonical explanation/model) is one where a model is composed of difference-making causal factors, such that the removal of a causal factor prevents the entailment of a phenomenon of interest. An idealization then is the introduction of a non-difference-making factor. For example, in modeling low-pressure gasses we often appeal to the ideal gas law, which assumes that gas molecules undergo no collisions. Although collisions do occur in low-pressure gasses, they do not make a difference to the essential character of ideal gas-like behavior (captured by the law). Importantly though, what counts as a minimal model will depend on the fineness of specification of the target itself. If, say, we were interested in explaining how low-pressure gasses diverge in behavior from an ideal gas, collisions may well become part of the key difference-making factors.

Still, due to the plethora of philosophical accounts of causation and explanation, there may be tension between the causal and explanatory aims of minimalist idealization. For instance, on the covering law account of explanation (Hempel and Oppenheim 1948 [1965]), one explains an explanandum by deriving it from a law along with initial and boundary conditions. A good candidate for a law in quantum theory is the Schrödinger equation and so, if the AB effect is understood narrowly as a shift in interference pattern due to an (almost) completely shielded magnetic field, then "the Schrödinger equation leads exactly to this prediction" (Magni and Valz-Gris 1995, 186). We thus have a kind of minimal model explanation of the AB effect. However, as is clear from the physics and philosophical controversy surrounding the AB effect, an identification of a covering-law explanation and difference-making factors does not seem sufficient for explaining the AB effect. Much of the debate in fact concerns the ontological causal basis of the AB effect: Is it due to a nonlocal magnetic field? Is the effect produced by the electromagnetic vector potential? Does the effect show that holonomies are physically significant? The issue is further problematized by the fact that such questions are intertwined both with foundationally interpretive issues (e.g., having to do with locality/nonlocality, determinism/indeterminism) and an understanding of the essential character of what the AB effect is in the first place (see Section 7).[9]

"Multiple-models idealization (hereafter MMI) is the practice of building multiple related but [possibly] incomplete models, each of which makes distinct claims about the nature and causal structure giving rise to a phenomenon" (Weisberg 2013, 103). MMI is governed by varying representational ideals so that one doesn't expect a single best model to be generated. For example, say we wish to both explain the ideal gas-type behavior of low-pressure gasses and make exceedingly precise predictions about the manner in which low-pressure gasses diverge in behavior from an ideal gas. It makes sense to use a minimalist idealization for the former and a

---

[9] Admittedly, since Weisberg's (2013) and Strevens's (2008) use of the minimal model generally concerns isolating difference-making *causal* factors, it may be odd to appeal to a seemingly noncausal account of explanation like the covering law account in order to give a minimal model explanation. However, Weisberg does intend his discussion to include the notion of the minimal model as it has been discussed by, say, Batterman (2002), and such a notion is noncausal. More generally, the tension I identify here arises given the many different philosophical accounts of causation and explanation. Of course, if by "explanation" one means causal explanation, and by "causal" one intends, say, a counterfactual account, then said tension will not arise.

Galilean idealization (with corresponding de-idealization techniques) for the latter. The point is that, due to the existence of trade-offs between different epistemic and pragmatic goals, for example, explanation and prediction, we need to appeal to MMI:

> The multiplicity of models is imposed by the contradictory demands of a complex and heterogeneous nature and a mind that can only cope with few variables at a time; by the contradictory desiderate of generality, realism, and precisions; by the need to understand and also to control; even by opposing esthetic standards which emphasize the stark simplicity and power of a general theories as against the richness and the diversity of living nature. These conflicts are irreconcilable. (Levins 1966, 27)

Hence, there are many motivations for introducing MMI. For instance, if one's goal is pedagogical it is reasonable to abide by the representational ideal of *simplicity*, where the idea is that we idealize away any irrelevant factors (even key causal ones) for the pedagogical exercise at hand. Or, if one is looking to maximize the number of *actual* or *possible* targets that an idealized model can represent, the *a-generality* and *p-generality* ideals, respectively, are called for. Importantly, explanatory and representational generalities stand in conflict with accurate and realistic representation, so trade-offs are associated with choosing between, say, the representational ideals of *1-causal* or *a-generality/p-generality* and the representational ideal of completeness:

> It is no theory that needs a new Hamiltonian for each new physical circum-stance. The explanatory power of quantum theory comes from its ability to deploy a small number of well-understood Hamiltonians to cover a wide range of cases. But this explanatory power has its price. If we limit the number of Hamiltonians, that is going to constrain our abilities to represent situations realistically (Cartwright 1983, 139).

Multiple-model idealization can also be introduced with one goal in mind, say, modeling key causal factors or maximizing prediction, when one cannot build a single model that contains all causal factors or maximizes predictive power.

Rohwer and Rice (2013) argue that Weisberg's three-fold taxonomy is missing an important fourth type of idealization, which they dub hypothetical patterns idealization (HPI), that aims to be explanatory but does not provide an explanation. The "motivation behind [HPI] is to construct models of hypothet-ical scenarios that, even though they may not accurately describe any core causal factors of a real-world system(s), are able to aid in the investigation of general patterns across extremely heterogeneous and complex systems" (Rohwer and Rice 2013, 344). In what sense is HPI explanatory then? Such idealization affords "how-possibly explanations," viz., it explains how a *general pattern* may *possibly* manifest. For instance, Rohwer and Rice describe how the Hawk–Dove model was constructed to show that restraint in combat between conspecifics is consistent with individual-level selection, viz., that it "is possible even in theory for individual selection to account for 'limited war' behavior" (Maynard Smith and Price 1973, 15). In fact, in Weisberg's (2013, Ch. 7) own discussion of "modeling without a specific target," he refers to Schelling's segregation model as giving a how-possibly explanation of how individual small preferences for like neighbors can "lead collectively to segregation" (Schelling 1978, 138).[10]

Even with HPI as a fourth type of idealization, is it doubtful that Weisberg's enhanced taxonomy can account for the different types and roles of idealizations. For example, let us consider whether idealizations I1–I3 in the AB effect, which instantiate a completely shielded magnetic field, are Galilean, minimalist, MMI, or HPI.[11] Although there is no doubt that I1–I3 simplify aspects of Aharonov and Bohm's (1959) derivation of the AB effect, such idealizations also significantly complexify matters due to underdetermination in their formal implementation (Shech 2018b). As Earman (2019, 2001) notes, "the simplification achieved by applying the idealizations [(I1)–(I3)] hides a seething complexity in the different ways the Hamiltonian operator can be made self-adjoint." That is to say, idealizations I1–I3 are *not solely* simplifying idealizations. Instead, they also complicate the situation because it turns out that there are many ways to formally implement I1–I3. Theorists are required to make a choice about the boundary conditions that obtain at the infinite solenoid boundary. We can think about these conditions as describing the manner by which the electron beam interacts with the solenoid border. In the non-idealized case, there is a *unique* dynamical evolution corresponding to the situation at hand and issues having to do with the formal implementation of I1–I3 need not arise. In the idealized case, however, there are different formal implementations of I1–I3, corresponding to different boundary conditions, which in turn correspond to diverse dynamics. Thus, idealizations I1–I3 are not Galilean idealizations.

Idealizations I1–I3 are also not introduced in order to set aside irrelevant factors and make salient the difference makers for the production and explanation of the AB effect, either narrowly construed as a shift in interference pattern or broadly construed as flux dependencies in the behavior of electrons. The key assumption used by Aharonov and Bohm (1959) is the AB *Ansatz*, and

---

[10] Also see Gelfert (2016) and Gelfert and Shech (2019) for a discussion of using models and idealizations, respectively, in order to provide "potential explanations."

[11] See Gelfert and Shech (2019) for a similar exercise using the examples of anyons and fractional statistics, and the Hubbard model of the Mott phase transition.

it is different from idealizations I1–I3. So idealizations I1–I3 are not minimalist idealizations. However, in Shech (2018) I argue that various rigorous results (e.g., de Oliveira and Pereira 2008, 2010, 2011; Ballesteros and Weder 2009, 2011) are needed to (partially) justify the choice of an idealized self-adjoint extension and can give a kind of minimal model explanation of the AB effect in the spirit of Batterman and Rice (2014). But the goal of such explanation is not to identify the key causal factors in the manifestation of the AB effect; it is to argue that various concrete physical systems can actually manifest the AB effect.

Regarding MMI, multiple models do arise in the AB effect case study in the form of multiple self-adjoint extensions of the original Hamiltonian for a charged particle in electromagnetic fields, resulting in many possible incompatible model-Hamiltonians available to represent the AB effect. However, the multiplicity of models does not conform to Weisberg's characterization of MMI as involving varying idealizations designed to serve different epistemic or pragmatic goals, which results from trade-offs between models. Neither do the multiple AB effect models work together as a group of Galilean or minimalist models to facilitate more precise predictions or a more complete picture of the causal factors involved, respectively.

Similarly, idealizations I1–I3 are not HPI since they are not appealed to in order to show that one could, in theory and possibly, explain the manifestation of the AB effect via the idealized description. Nonetheless, Shech and Gelfert (2019) have argued that one possible idealization in fiber bundle formulation of the AB effect, in which the AB effect is a manifestation of a literal hole in physical space that does not exist in actual laboratory setting (viz., a non-simply connected base space), can generate a potential explanation of the effect. Whether or not such a potential explanation ought to be upgraded to a how-possibly explanation depends on one's views on such explanations, viz., on whether something that is nomically possible but contingently/practically impossible counts as a genuine possibility. In any case, idealizing physical space itself to have a hole does not concern idealizations I1–I3 that we have been discussing.

What roles do idealizations I1–I3 play in the AB effect? As argued in Shech (2018b, 2022a), Shech and Gelfert (2019), and Earman (2019), I1–I3 are best interpreted as facilitating scientific exploration (Gelfert 2016), such as exploring the modal structure of quantum theory and the contrast with classical physics, which directly affords a deeper understanding of quantum theory and of what the AB effect is in the first place, as well as an indirect understanding of why the AB effect manifests (say) in the laboratory (Shech 2022a). Thus, Weisberg's enhanced taxanomy "is lacking in that it does not make room for the exploratory role of idealizations and models, thereby offering a distorted view of the case studies" like the AB effect (Shech and Gelfert 2019, 196).

An additional type of "idealization," which possibly does not clearly fit with Weisberg's enhance taxonomy, is one that ostensibly allows scientists to get at the true nature of phenomena. The idea is captured in the following quote by Ellis (1992, 266):

> Physical science ... is fundamentally concerned to discover the essential natures of the kinds of things that can exist ... in a world such as ours. And to achieve its aims, science must focus on the intrinsic properties and structures of the basic kind of things and processes which are to be found existing or occurring in nature.
>
> In pursuit of its aims, it is necessary for science to abstract from the accidental properties of things, and the extrinsic forces which act upon them, to consider how they would behave independently of these properties, or in the absence of these forces. For this is the only way of finding out what behavior is generated by the intrinsic properties and structures of the kinds of things we are studying, and what is due to other extraneous influences ... The aim of science ... is to explain what happens by showing how what occurs can be seen to arise out of the essential natures of the natural kinds and processes which constitute the real world.

It is beyond our scope to evaluate the worldview encapsulated by talk of "essential natures of the natural kinds and processes," but it certainly does seem like Ellis's view that idealization is a "necessary device for conceptually isolating the natural processes which are the main subject matter of our inquiries" (1992, 281) is meant to convey something stronger than Weisberg's and Stevens's notion of a minimalist idealization as making salient the difference-making factors for the occurrence of phenomenon. One may object that no additional type of idealization is needed since it is Ellis's particular metaphysical views, instead of something about idealization per se, which grounds the need for the alleged additional type of idealization. Still, if indeed natural kinds and process have essential natures, and idealization allows us to abstract away from accidental properties in a way not accounted for by minimalist idealizations, Ellis's characterization would remain an additional type of idealization.

One way to develop this idea is to view idealization as a process that facilitates our focusing on particular *scales* of interest, and those scales contain real entities and behaviors that are of interest to scientists. As noted in Section 2, "there seems to be interesting physics at all scales" (Georgi 1993, 210). Such sentiments and related case studies suggest a particular view about ontology and scales. For example, Ladyman and Ross (2007) hold the view that "ontology is scale-relative, in the sense that different energy levels and regimes, as well as different length and time scales, feature different emergent structures of causation and law" (Ladyman 2018, 103). Shech and McGivern (2021, 1412) similarly argue that "ontology is scale dependent," and that in the fractional quantum Hall effect the theory, at "the high-energy scale, neglects the emergent entities and behaviors that are doing all the explanatory work."[12]

The idea can be generally conveyed in the context of QFT:

> [Imagine] that you have a QFT with lots of different particles with widely varying masses. In situations where there isn't enough energy to create a certain particle, parts of the theory which make reference to that particle can be ignored. Thus, at such low energies, physics is described by an [EFT] which 'effectively' captures everything relevant. (Huggett and Weingard 1995, 172)

But wording the issue in such a manner does seem to suggest that the notion of a minimalist idealization is at play here. Moreover, it may be objected that, if entities and behaviors at low-energy scales are "real," then it isn't clear in what sense their representation is an "idealization." One possible way around such a worry would be to appeal to Potochnik's (2017) view that phenomena are causally complex and thus embody (possibly infinitely) many patterns of interest. Idealizations then "are used to set aside complicating factors to help scientist discern the causal patterns they are primarily interested in" (Potochnik 2017, 47).

More generally, Potochnik (2017) provides three on-point critiques of Weisberg's taxonomy. First, she notes that, in most cases in science, there will be many motivations for idealizing and so MMI "will apply to most all instances of idealization," but since MMI "is not defined by a single representational ideal," and, since such "ideals were supposed to demarcate the different kinds of idealization," Weisberg's account loses much of its force (45). Second, she presents a kind of dilemma: MMI can be understood narrowly or broadly. Narrow characterizations will have the implication that the taxonomy leaves out important types of idealization (such as HPI and exploratory idealizations), while broadly construed "the category of [MMI] is so broad that it is a sort of dustbin category, uninformative about the features of idealizations that fall into it" (46). Still, Weisberg has a ready reply to both worries, namely that his account need not be interpreted to be exhaustive. We can then construe MMI narrowly and add additional interesting types of idealizations to the taxonomy.

It is here that Potochnik's third critique pulls weight: A "taxonomy of kinds of idealizations presents as defined categories what are better understood as overlapping motivations for idealizing ... [Instead] of discrete kinds of idealization motivated by distinct representational aims, there are many intertwined reasons to idealize ... the list of reasons to idealize is open-ended" (47).[13]

---

[12] See Sections 5–6.   [13] Compare Table 2.

If indeed reasons and motivations for idealizing form a kind of overlapping continuum instead of finite and discrete sets, then taxonomies like Weisberg's will give a distorted picture of the practice and role of idealization. Deciding which view of idealization is correct is difficult, though, because it depends on one's more general epistemic and ontological views of science and the world as, for example, the Ellis quote suggests.

4 Justification

A repeated claim made in the literature is that there are many justifications for idealization and that de-idealization concerns only Galilean idealizations, which are introduced for temporary computational expedience. For instance, Weisberg (2013) claims that minimalist idealization "should be justified with respect to the cognitive role played by minimal models: They aid in scientific explanations" (102). Also, multiple representational ideals notwithstanding, he says that "one especially important justification of MMI is the existence of tradeoffs" (103), and that MMI "is not justified by the possibility of de-idealization back to the full representation."

Potochnik (2017) says that some reasons "justify the incorporation of an idealization merely temporarily [e.g., in working with *completeness*], and others justify permanent idealization" and that this "decides whether de-idealization will ever be warranted" (48). In fact, she claims that some idealizations can be justified "in virtue of mundane reasons as a research's previous training in modeling technique that she then attempts to apply to unrelated phenomena" (49) and that idealizations are not only rampant in science but *unchecked*: viz., "that there is little focus on eliminating idealizations or even controlling their influence" (42).

To my mind, such sentiments suggest a conflation here between our *reasons*, motives, goals, and aims for (as well as what we hope to get out of) introducing idealization into science and scientific representation, and the idea that idealization ought to be *justified*, that we have an epistemic-logical debt to discharge by explaining why an idealization works. Explanatory goals, pragmatic concerns, the existence of trade-offs, and so forth are *reasons* for appealing to idealizations, not justifications for doing so. In fact, reliable and accurate predictions and explanations based on highly idealized representations should strike one as miraculous and mind-boggling, unless one has a story to tell about how the factors relevant for said prediction and explanation are represented realistically, truthfully, and accurately in order to afford such prediction and explanation. Importantly, in-principle de-idealization broadly construed, hereafter de-idealization, is exactly that type of story. For example, in the context of scientific modelling it is standardly claimed:

> A ... model contains an idealization when it correctly describes some of the ... factors at work, but falsely assumes that other factors that affect the outcome are absent. The idealizations in a ... model are harmless if correcting them [via de-idealization] wouldn't make much difference in the predicted value of the effect variable. Harmless idealizations can be explanatory. (Elgin and Sober 2002, 448)[14]

In this section, I try to bring this point to light by discussing the need to justify idealizations in the context of prediction and explanation, and by interacting critically with a contextualist proposal suggested by Kevin Davey (2011) for how justified beliefs can be generated from idealizations.

Consider the notion of prediction and say that you would like to make predictions about the behavior of low-pressure gasses. For pragmatic reasons like convenience, you could appeal to the simple ideal gas law: $PV = nRT$, where P is pressure, V volume, T temperature, R the ideal gas constant, and n the number of gas molecules in units of moles (viz., the number of gas molecules divided by Avogadro's constant). Now consider that you also are interested in making predictions about a gas at higher pressures. Typically, the ideal gas law fails at making correct predictions for such situations. For example, using the ideal gas law for a low-pressure scenario, for one mole of carbon dioxide gas at standard temperature $273.15\,K$ and a volume of $22.4\,L$, the pressure will be $P = 1\,atm$. If we now de-idealize by recalculating the pressure using the more realistic Van der Waals equation, we would see that $P = 0.996\,atm$, which is roughly $1\,atm$. But shrink your gas-in-a-box to a volume of $0.224\,L$ (thereby raising the pressure), and the ideal gas law predicts a pressure of $P = 100$ atm, while the Van der Waals equation gives $P = 52$ atm. With higher pressures we can no longer ignore molecular interaction and treat all collision as elastic (as we do in the ideal gas model) if we are interested in accurate predictions.

One manner by which the issue of *justification* can enter this scenario is in the way of accounting for how an unrealistic model like an ideal gas could provide accurate predictions for low-pressure gasses. We want to know what justifies the use of a "false" model in making correct predictions. One can thus *de-idealize* to the more realistic Van der Waals equation and show that predictions based on both models are approximately the same. This is similar to what inter-theoretic

---

[14] Similar sentiments can be found in, for example, Earman (2004), Mäki (1994), McMullin (1985), Potochnik (2017), Ruetsche (2011), Strevens (2008), Weisberg (2013), and Woodward (2003).

reduction affords us on the level of theories. For example, why does the classical Newton expression for momentum $p = mv$ work so well for everyday-sized objects and temporal scales when it is based on a "false" theory? Because in the domain of everyday-sized objects and temporal scales, objects typically move at velocities much smaller than the speed of light, and in the low-velocity limit of

$v/c \to 0$, the more accurate special relativistic expression of $p = mv / \sqrt{1 - \dfrac{v^2}{c^2}}$

is approximately equal to $p = mv$.

Returning to the gas-in-a-box case, imagine that no de-idealization to some more realistic scenario was possible in principle. When we attempt to de-idealize by, say, constructing the Van der Waals model and putting it to the test, it gives us wrong predictions. Such a result should move us to seriously reexamine our theories and alleged understanding of gasses. Similarly, imagine that the ideal gas law was able to generate predictions that were both reliable and as accurate as the Van der Waals model even for gasses at high pressures. What would we make of this scenario? Reliability means that such predictions are not flukes. Thus, either such reliable prediction ought to be taken as miraculous and mysterious, as if we were using a magic 8-ball to make reliable predictions, or else one could reasonably infer that, contrary to expectations, the factors taken into account in the Van der Waals equation such as intermolecular attraction and volume excluded by moles of molecules, are *not* difference makers for the thermodynamic behavior of high-pressure gasses. Such findings would likely necessitate a significant alteration to our theories of gasses.

Another manner by which the issue of justification arises has to do with whether we could have justified beliefs if they are based on arguments and calculations that appeal to falsities in the way of idealizations. Consider a different example where a physicist wants to calculate the radius of the helical path traveled by a small, charged particle fired at an angle into a long cylindrical tube, around which a current-carrying wire has been tightly wrapped. As Davey (2011, 17) notes, typically one will appeal to various idealizations in making such calculations: we assume that the cylinder is infinitely long, the wire is infinitely thin and wound infinitely tightly, the current is constant, and so forth. Such idealizations allow physicists to argue that the magnetic field inside the cylinder is uniform.

In turn, the radius of the particle's path is determined by applying the Lorentz force law and our physicist comes to conclusion C' that "the radius of the helical motions is approximately r" based on premises $P_1 \ldots P_n$, which encompass the Lorentz law and the various idealized assumptions. But this leads to the following puzzle: Given that some of premises $P_1 \ldots P_n$ are false (due to their idealized nature), so that one is not generally justified in believing $P_1 \ldots P_n$, how can such an inferential basis generate *justified* belief in C'? What is key to notice is that prediction is inferential: when we predict, we make inferences based on theories, models, observations, data gathered, and so forth, and inferences based on false premises are usually not warranted.[15]

Such worries can be extended to cases where idealizations are used to give explanations. For example, on a covering law account of explanation, $P_1 \ldots P_n$ would *fail* to constitute an explanation of C', since "the sentences constituting the explanans must be true" (Hempel and Oppenheim 1948 [1965: 248]) and some of $P_1 \ldots P_n$ are not true because idealization is involved. Of course there is a literature large enough to merit a book of its own focusing on issues concerning idealization and explanation, such as whether explanation must be veridical, and idealization and understanding, such as whether understanding is factive. Other than my brief treatment in Section 7, such issues are beyond the scope of this Element. Still, the point is that, in the same way that convenience and tractability for predictive purposes are reasons but not justifications for idealization, explanation and the existence of trade-offs are reasons and not justifications for idealization.

Moreover, *justification* for appealing to idealization *is* provided by de-idealization. For instance, if it possible to de-idealize $P_1 \ldots P_n$ and arrive at a non-idealized set of true claims $P'_1 \ldots P'_n$ about a particle shot into a solenoid such that $P'_1 \ldots P'_n$ imply the conclusion C' that "the radius of the helical motions is approximately r," then we will be justified in believing C'. Similarly, we saw that de-idealization facilitates an explanation and thus justification for why one can appeal to an idealized model (e.g., the ideal gas model) or theory (e.g., Newtonian physics) when it is, strictly speaking, false or inaccurate. Nevertheless, one may object that the need for a justifying idealization only arises if it is assumed that science aims at truth (Potochnik 2017, ch. 4), or if some sort of scientific realism or veridicality about explanation is presupposed (Sections 5 and 6). But idealizations are used to make inferences and produce justified beliefs – for example, in the context of prediction/retrodiction, deduction/derivation, providing explanations or representations, affording understanding – and, again, *inferences are generally not warranted if they are based on false propositions or beliefs.*

In any case, it is worthwhile to note that "de-idealization" here is intended to be broadly construed to include any story and technique one may appeal to in order to provide the required epistemic-logical justification such as robustness analysis (Levins 1966; Weisberg 2013, ch. 9), perturbation theory and

---

[15] Generally, this holds both for deductive and nondeductive – that is, ampliative-inductive – inferences.

dimensional analysis (Pincock 2020), demotion of idealization to approximation (Norton 2012; Shech 2015b, 2018b), appeals to upscaling and homogen-
ization (Batterman 2021; Homes 2022), and appeals to universality (Gryb et al.
2021; Rice 2021).

Let us consider the last example. Define the "order parameter" Ψ for some
fluid-in-a-box, say, oxygen O_2, to be the difference between the densities of the
liquid ρ_l and the vapor ρ_v states: $\Psi = |\rho_l - \rho_v|$. It turns out that, experimentally,
if we plot the reduced temperature T/T_c as a function of the reduced density
P/P_c, we attain a (best fit) curve with a shape described by the relation $\Psi \propto \epsilon^\beta$,
where β is the "critical exponent," T_c and P_c the so-called critical temperature
and critical pressure, respectively, and $\epsilon = |(T_c - T)/T|$ is a measure of how
close a system is to the critical temperature. Now, say that you want to
theoretically calculate β and, rather than doing so with the Hamiltonian (or
Lagrangian) corresponding to the fluid O_2 (i.e., what we take to be a more
"realistic" representation our target), you radically idealize the situation at hand
and calculate β with the Hamiltonian for the fluid nitrogen N_2 or neon N_e. Or
you appeal to an even a more radical idealization in which you use the
Hamiltonian for a ferromagnet (where the order parameter concerns the net
magnetization).

As it turns out, near the critical temperature and pressure, doing so will afford
you a correct prediction for β. But what justifies such radical idealization? The
justification comes in the form of the renormalization group (RG) explanation
of critical phenomena, which, for our purposes, is basically an explanation of
how all said Hamiltonians are in the same "universality class." This means that
all such systems share critical exponents that are decided by properties such as
the dimension and symmetry of the target system's Hamilton (see Figure 6). The
point is that appealing to an RG explanation of the sort also counts as a kind of in
principle de-idealization argument and de-idealization ought to be interpreted in
a broad manner.[16] Namely, one can justifiably use "idealized" Hamiltonians to
derive universal properties like critical exponents since some RG argument
guarantees that less idealized Hamiltonians in the same universality class will
lead to the same results.

As an additional example, recall the case of Brownian motion (Section 1). In
explaining his application of classical hydrodynamics to a heterogenous
molecular system that is idealized to be homogenous (viz., rigid spherical
sugar molecule suspended in a fluid water solvent) Einstein says:

---

[16] Of course, I'm conveniently ignoring the fact that RG explanations themselves appeal to
idealizations of sorts vis-à-vis the thermodynamic limit and infinite RG transformations. See
footnote 21.

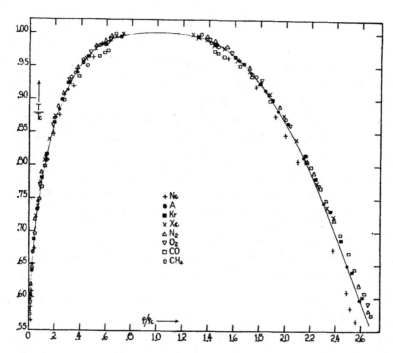

Figure 6 Universality of critical phenomena (Guggenheim 1945, 256)

[If] the volume of a molecule of the solute is large compared with the volume of a molecule of the solvent [then] ... such a solute molecule will behave approximately, with respect to its mobility in the solvent, and in respect to its influence on the viscosity of the latter, as a solid body suspended in the solvent, and it will be allowable to apply to the motion of the solvent in the immediate neighborhood of a molecule the hydrodynamic equations, in which the liquid is considered homogeneous, and, accordingly, its molecular structure is ignored. (Einstein 1926/1956, 36–37)

Thus, Einstein justifies representing a heterogenous system with an idealized homogenous system by arguing that "the actual heterogeneous lower-scale details of the solute-solvent are basically irrelevant" (Batterman 2021).

All this is to say, we must not conflate the *reasons* for appealing to idealization (in light of some goals like prediction, explanation, description, etc.) with the *justification* given for how such goals could be legitimately achieved in spite of (or in virtue of) idealization. There is a need to justify idealization and de-idealization, if possible, and to the extent relevant for the goal at hand, affords such justification. Such insights suggest endorsing the following principle by John Earman:

Earman's Sound Principle. "While idealizations are useful and, perhaps, even essential to progress in physics, a sound principle of interpretation would seem to be that no effect can be counted as a genuine physical effect if it disappears when the idealizations are removed" (Earman, 2004, 191).

However, what may count as an idealization in the context of current theory may be regarded as a realistic description in future theory, and vice versa. For instance, in the seventeenth century in which the corpuscular theory of light was well received, modeling light as a wave would be considered an idealization. With the shift to the wave theory of light cemented by the beginning of the nineteenth century, such wave models would be taken to be realistic. By the mid-twentieth century, however, with the advent and development of quantum theory, both models of light as a particle or wave can be considered idealizations. Thus, Laura Ruetsche has suggested that the following principle is more apt.

> *Ruetsche's Sounder Principle.* "No effect predicted by a non-final theory can be counted as a genuine physical effect if it disappears and stays disappeared from that theory's successors" (2011, 336).

Although the emphasis here is on the physical significance of alleged effects (like the AB effect), predicted by theory or model, both principles seem to take de-idealization as the general justificatory grounds for idealizations. They suggest that explanations and/or predictions of effects arising in target systems of interest, which are based on indispensable idealizations, are, at best, suspect, and, at worst, illegitimate.

But if de-idealization plays such a central role in justifying idealizations, is it generally possible to de-idealize the various idealizations that arise in science? Or, as Potochnik holds, are idealizations in science "unchecked" such that "there is little focus on eliminating idealizations or even controlling their influence"? (42). Are some idealizations indispensable in the sense that they can't be de-idealized?[17] Let us consider such questions in the context of the aforementioned example concerning the radius of the helical path traveled by a charged particle, in which a set of premises $P_1 \ldots P_n$, some of which are idealized and some of which concern laws, allow us to come to the conclusion C' that "the radius of the helical motions is approximately r." If we are generally not justified in believing C', on the basis of an argument A' that is constituted by $P_1 \ldots P_n$, then a revised argument A^* that includes de-idealization may afford justification in the following manner (Davey 2011, 20):

1. State the laws of electromagnetism (Maxwell's equations) and any other laws to be used in the remainder of the argument.
2. Argue that if the usual ideal assumptions are made about the solenoid, the resulting radius of the helical motion will be exactly r.

---

[17] See chapters 5 and 6 for ostensible examples.

3. Argue that by adding small but bounded width to the wires, small but bounded inhomogeneities in the current, and so on, one gets a small but bounded difference in the radius of motion. Calculate the largest size δr of an "error" that might be introduced in this way to the previous calculation of the radius, and infer that the radius of the particle lies in the range $(r - \delta r, r + \delta r)$.

Steps 1–2 justify the inference from $P_1 \ldots P_n$ to the conclusion C that "the radius of the helical motions is exactly r," but C holds for the idealized scenario. De-idealization occurs in step 3 and justifies the conclusion C^* that "the radius of the helical motions is $r \pm \delta r$," which is one manner by which to justify and flesh out C'. Davey (2011, 20) calls proposals that attempt to justify inferences and beliefs based on idealization by appealing to arguments like A^*, which involve explicit de-idealization, *mathematico-deductive* "because it allows us to calculate the approximate radius r by applying only valid mathematical and deductive forms of argument to statements about the laws of nature and the approximate initial state of our system." So, what is wrong with the mathematico-deductive proposal?

Davey puts forth three main charges against the mathematico-deductive proposal and all concern problems with de-idealization in some way. First, he notes that the only known method for explicitly writing down an argument like A^*, i.e., the only known method of de-idealization, is one where "we assume that the actual system differs from the ideal system in very specific and ideal ways" (21). For example, we can introduce a small, semicircular "bump" in portions of the wire in order to represent inhomogeneities and we can calculate the effect such a bump will have on the motion of the particle (see Figure 7). But such de-idealization involves further idealization.

Second, theories like classical electromagnetism are themselves idealized and thus incomplete in important ways that impede giving an argument like A^*. For instance, it is well known that Maxwell's equations cannot account for the stability of matter so A^* will also have as its conclusion that no stable matter exists. This point generalizes: most target systems are studied and represented with theories and models that are incomplete such that genuine de-idealization involves appealing to *other* theories and models. However, at this juncture a

Figure 7 Ideal deviation from ideality

third problem arises. Namely, science itself is incomplete and so the de-idealization process will end prematurely before an argument like A^* can even possibly arise. For example, we could solve the issue of the stability of matter by appealing to quantum theory but genuine de-idealization would also include an account of how gravitational attraction has only a negligible effect on aspects of our target system. The problem, then, is that an argument like A^* "is impossible to make using only laws of nature in which we currently have justified belief because no sufficiently well-developed theory of quantum gravity exists" (22).

As an alternative, Davey (2011, 23) considers an *inductive proposal* for argument A^* with the aim of justifying the idealizations involved. In particular, imagine that our physicist conducts a great number of experiments and discovers that the actual trajectories of charged particles in solenoids are indeed approximately like the ones calculated from theory. An inductive proposal for A^* suggests itself:

1. Point out the inductive evidence that suggests that charged particles in carefully constructed solenoids behave like ideal particles in ideal solenoids.
2. Calculate the exact radius r of the helical motion of an appropriately chosen ideal particle traveling through an appropriately chosen ideal solenoid.
3. Conclude that the radius of motion in the actual case is approximately r.

Step 2 justifies the inference from $P_1 \ldots P_n$ to the conclusion C but, again, C holds for the idealized scenario. Step 1 fills the gap of de-idealization by providing justificatory inductive evidence supporting the inference from C to conclusion C'. But does the inductive proposal for A^* justify belief in C'? Davey claims that it does, but admits that, "if we want to say (as … we should) that the calculation shows the physicist why r has the rough value it does, then we must view the physicist as doing something more than merely exploiting a reliable method of belief formation" (23–24). That is to say, the inductive proposal does not satisfactorily *explain* how the physicist manages to generate justified belief.[18]

The failures of the mathematico-deductive and inductive proposals led Davey (2011) to suggest his own contextualist proposal for the justification of idealization. Setting many details aside, the basic idea is that the truth conditions for propositions like $P_1 \ldots P_n$ are dependent on a set of (objective but sometimes shifting) standards – criteria employed by a community for the attribution of properties to objects. It therefore follows that, in spite of idealization, and *relative to an appropriate set of standards*, $P_1 \ldots P_n$ and C are "true," and we are justified in believing C based on $P_1 \ldots P_n$ in the usual manner:

---

[18] Also, without additional background information about our target system, I do not think that pure enumerative induction can play the justificatory role that Davey suggests (Shech 2019c, 2022b).

> According to the everyday standards of classical electrodynamics . . . it is true that the solenoid is a finite cylinder of uniformly circulating charge, and it is true that the charged particle fired into it is a point particle with some particular charge and mass. Applied to physical systems of this sort . . . using the standards appropriate for calculations in macroscopic electrodynamics, Maxwell's equations and the Lorentz force law are true. Thus, we may apply these laws to our system in the usual textbook manner . . . So we are justified in believing that the particle will move in a helical trajectory with a given radius, and moreover, we are justified in believing that this will happen precisely because our mathematical calculation makes a sequence of true claims (relative to certain standards). Our result is not merely the output of a reliable mechanism of belief formation – instead, the calculation is explanatory and shows in a straightforward way why the result is mathematically forced on us. (Davey 2011, 30–31)

What are we to make of Davey's (2011) analysis? To begin, Davey's identification of the great extent to which idealization arises on virtually every level of scientific inquiry confirms the claim made many times over that idealization in science is rampant. His analysis also brings to light the importance of justifying idealization – of giving an explanation of why idealized descriptions, theories, and models work – and not conflating the reasons given for idealization with justification. It isn't clear to me, however, that the move toward contextualism can provide the sought-for justification.

Consider his claim that $P_1 \ldots P_n$ and C are "true" relative to the everyday standards of classical electrodynamics. What determines this and how do we know that this is the case? Insofar as we appeal to some sort of purely enumerative inductive evidence – say, we note that given different standards of measurement precision, charged particles in the laboratory behave like standard-free ideal particles in ideal solenoids – we seem to be back at a version of the inductive proposal. Instead, if we appeal to explicit de-idealization – say, we note that given various reasonable standards of accuracy all calculated particle radii lie in the range $(r - \delta r, r + \delta r)$ – then we are back at a version of the mathematico-deductive proposal.

Davey, for instance, says that it "would probably be stretching things . . . to say that [it is true that] the cylinder is infinitely long relative to [the aforementioned] standards" (2011, page 31, note 5). Why is this the case? In virtue of what exactly is it the case that, relative to the everyday standards of classical electrodynamics, a solenoid is a finite cylinder of uniformly circulating charge but it isn't infinitely long? Davey notes that by "the everyday standards of classical electrodynamics" he really means a large cluster of standards bound together with a commitment to ostensible ontology of the theory – for example, things like point charges, well-defined charge distributions, and continuous current densities. Still, my point is that without appeal to de-idealization broadly construed (to include a host of techniques as noted above), it is both difficult to determine what standards like "the everyday standards of classical electrodynamics" really amount to, and to understand how we can know whether some proposition is indeed true relative to a set standard. De-idealization, say, as it arises in limiting relations between models and theories, also facilitates identifying the limits and domains of models and theories. We know we need not worry about the stability-of-matter problem in solving problems of classical electromagnetism because quantum theory comes to the rescue. Although we have no accepted theory of quantum gravity, classical gravitational theory itself is helpful in identifying its limits and domain, giving us good reasons to think that the effect of gravity on charged particles in and constituting solenoids is negligible.

Moreover, as Davey admits, his account focuses on the "simplest cases of idealization" and is too undeveloped to deal with more exotic cases (32). For instance, concentrating on the AB effect as it manifests in the laboratory, is it true – given the standards appropriate for semiclassical representation of a quantum particle in classical electromagnetic fields – that the magnetic field is completely shielded? Ought the standard AB effect setup to be understood as a literally true description of laboratory experiments given the appropriate standards? If yes, it isn't clear how to make sense of the historical debate surrounding the AB effect as proponents of the controversy seem to explicitly question what quantum theory predicts about idealized scenarios with the goal of shedding light of foundational issues (Section 7, Shech 2022a). If no, the shift to contextualism does not help us understand how such idealizations facilitate justified inferences.

Crucially, it isn't at all clear what standards we are supposed to appeal to given the semiclassical framework at play and the fact that both classical electromagnetism and QM concern large clusters of conflicting standards. Moreover, QM admits of varying interpretations that in turn may suggest varying sets of (likely conflicting) standards (e.g., on the orthodox interpretation an object's position may be indeterminate while on the Bohmian interpretation it is determinate). Generally, statements that are "mixed," viz., where some terms ought to be evaluated relative to one standard and other terms relative to another, may not be semantically well formed.

In any case, none of this is meant to offer a definitive criticism of Davey's approach. However, as it stands, it isn't clear that talk of standards allows us to do away with the role that de-idealization plays in justifying idealization since it seems that de-idealization will aid in deciding both which standards are reasonable to choose and whether propositions are true/false relative to chosen standards. Furthermore, reflecting on his charges against the mathematico-deductive approach, I worry that Davey's dismissal is too quick. Regarding the first charge, it is true that any argument A^* "that we can *actually* write down still involves idealized assumptions" (21; my emphasis). But what matters for justifying inferences based on idealizations is that we have good reasons for believing that, in principle, de-idealization is possible. That said, what does seem to be missing is a developed discussion of what the "in principle" versus "in practice" distinction amounts to, and a worked-out account of what type of in-principle de-idealization can provide the justificatory grounds. For instance, insofar as de-idealization fails because a theory's predicted effect disappears when idealizations are removed, or it disappears and stays disappeared from that theory's successors, then it seems that such an effect is an artifact of idealization and ought not to be counted as a genuine physical effect. But what if, as a matter of fact about current science, our best theories of some phenomena involve idealization (Sections 5 and 6)? Is the presence of such idealization principled or practical?

For example, our best theories (including RG explanations) of phase transitions (PT) turn out to involve appeals to the thermodynamic limit (TDL) (in which particle number and volume diverge while density remains constant), and such a limit is an idealization (broadly construed).[19] There is, of course, no in-principle argument against developing PT theories that don't appeal to the idealized TDL. In fact, attempts have been made at developing exactly such theories (Ardourel 2018; Menon and Callender 2013). Still, to my knowledge, no theories-without-the-TDL are as successful at predicting and explaining critical exponents as theories-with-the-TDL.

Does this mean that de-idealization is "in principle" impossible?[20] Or is it just "in practice?" On one hand, practical impediments can typically be solved with enough time and computational power, but it isn't clear that this is applicable to the case of PT theories-without-the-TDL. There is a difference, for instance, between noting that given enough time (perhaps millions of years) one can calculate the trajectory of some n-body problem for some given time interval, and between holding that given enough time we are optimistic that scientists will construct theories-without-the-TDL of PT that are as successful as theories-with-the-TDL. The former case concerns a practical issue, but it isn't clear that the latter does too. On the other hand, there's nothing along the lines of a "no-go theorem" that is applicable to theories-without-the-TDL.

The situation is somewhat similar to Pincock's (2020, 5) discussion of essentially idealized models in which "a model is essentially idealized when any model of that type with that purpose has an idealization of some kind . . . and there is no

---

[19] Also, even on Norton's (2012) narrow construal, *some* versions of the TDL are idealizations instead of approximations.

[20] Of course, one could attempt to directly de-idealize RG explanations – see Palacios (2019) and Wu (2021) for such a suggestion.

known way to [fulfill said purpose] without using a model with that kind of idealization" (my emphasis). A "model is not essentially idealized when each idealization of the model can be avoided in a way that preserves the intended modelling purpose." In such cases, it isn't clear whether the impediment to de-idealization ought to be considered in-principle or in-practice. Namely, if there *currently* is no "known" way to avoid some idealization, does this suggest no way to avoid such idealization in the *future*? Perhaps, given the history of scientific research on a particular target, or history of scientific success more generally, we have reasons to be optimistic or pessimistic about the developments of theories and models that can clearly be de-idealized. Historical inductions, though, are fraught with difficulties (Shech 2019c).

Another example (concerning ostensible indispensable idealizations pertaining to current theories) has to do with the notion of strong emergence. Strong emergence is understood as an in-principle failure of reduction, i.e., an in-principle failure to derive or deduce some sought-after result with the reducing base or theory (Chalmers 2006). Perhaps, as Palacios (2022) argues, the in-principle/in-practice distinction is not a fruitful manner by which to think about emergence/reduction in particular. Still, the back-and-forth debate regarding in-principle/in-practice derivability may be helpful for understanding the distinction's role in justifying idealizations.

For instance, in discussing whether the properties of higher-level (macro) condensed-matter systems are consequences of the properties of their lower-level (micro) atomic-level components, Leggett (1992, 227) says that "no significant advance in the theory of matter in bulk has ever come about through derivation from microscopic principles" and that it "is *in principle and forever impossible* to carry out such a derivation." On the other hand, one can view many theories of condensed-matter systems as EFTs (Bain 2013), and it has been argued that "[any] facts or predictions (or collectively, truths) obtained via the EFT, no matter how unexpected or seemingly disconnected from the lower-level point of view, is in principle deducible from the lower-level domain" (Luu and Meißner 2019, 7–8). Others hold that "one cannot in an easy way state that EFTs disprove" in-principle failure of reducibility (Ellis 2020, 1133). Ellis's basic claim seems to be that higher-level/macro systems are governed by dynamics that are altered with respect to the low-level/micro descriptions so that one cannot derive the former from the latter without knowing ahead of time which higher-level dynamics are needed. For instance, in the context of symmetry breaking he says:

> [You] have to add a symmetry breaking term into the micro theory in order to get the correct macro theory, because it's not there in the fundamental physics; but you only can work out what symmetry breaking term to add

from your knowledge of the correct macro theory. You have to use variables
defined by that higher level theory to get the symmetry broken effective micro
theory which gives the correct macro result. (Ellis 2020, 1111)

However, for the purpose of justifying idealizations in the form of an EFT (or
for deciding on issues of emergence/reduction), "in-principle derivation"
shouldn't mean "in-principle derivation without knowledge of the correct
macro results." In any case, my point is that insofar as in-principle de-idealization
plays a justificatory role for idealization, and given that the in-principle/in-
practice distinction isn't always clear-cut, some work is needed to identify
whether, in specific cases, de-idealization is possible to the extent needed for
justification.

As for Davey's second charge, I don't see the problem with admitting that a
theory or model has a limited domain of application and that, if problematic
issues (such as the instability/stability of matter) arise, we ought to appeal to
other theories and models. This isn't an in-principle impediment to de-
idealization. But Davey's discussion does bring to light how the notions of
idealization and de-idealization are bound together with commitments to
interpretation of theory and its ontology. For instance, as part of the second
charge he notes that we tend to view the electric current as something that is
flowing uniformly through the wire, even though a current is a flow of a
swarm of electrons, which are likely moving in slightly different directions
(21–22). In order to appeal to the notions of idealization/de-idealization in
this context we need to first interpret what classical electromagnetism tells us
the world is like, e.g., that currents are really just swarms of electrons, that
electrons are point particles. This is the basis for identifying a uniform current
as an idealization that needs to be justified via de-idealization, which in turn
may necessitate investigating and appealing to other relevant theories and
models. It is also true that, as per the third charge, de-idealization may end
prematurely since science is incomplete. Such incompleteness contributes to
the overall evidential debt that comes about in doing science – since all
inferences based on scientific theories, models, and evidence are, ultimately,
ampliative-inductive, our conclusions may be false. But that isn't to say that
they aren't justified.

Last, it may be more fruitful to think of the inductive proposal as complementary to the mathematico-deductive one. The fact that inductive evidence
suggests that charged particles in carefully constructed solenoids behave like
ideal particles in ideal solenoids confirms that explicit de-idealization methods
are fulfilling their justificatory role. After all, if charged particles behaved
radically different from ideal particles, and such departures form ideality

couldn't be accounted for via de-idealization, it would give us good reason to reconsider our theoretical understanding of such target systems. Similarly, Davey's own contexualist proposal may be viewed as complementary to the (now enhanced) mathematico-deductive-inductive proposal, wherein issues of scale-relative ontology arise. Recall that Ladyman and Ross (2007) and Shech and McGivern (2021) have suggested that there is a sense in which descriptions of targets in terms of non-fundamental entities (like electrical currents), which are dependent on but nonetheless autonomous from their constituents (like electrons), are "true" instead of idealized.[21] Davey's account allows us to make sense of this idea, viz., such descriptions are true relative to the standards decided by the scale in which a phenomenon and its explanation arises.

In conclusion, I maintain that we ought not conflate reasons for introducing idealizations (Table 2) with the justification that needs to be supplied given the epistemic-logical debt incurred by appeals to idealizations. Such justification is required because, regardless of our aims and goals, irrespective of whether we are interested in theories or models, and in spite of the plethora of types of models, accounts of explanation, and so forth, idealizations are used to make inferences and inferences are generally not warranted if they are based on false propositions. In principle de-idealization, broadly construed, provides the sought-after justification but it isn't always clear that such de-idealization is, in principle, possible; nor it is completely clear how to draw the line between in principle and in practice de-idealization in terms of the justificatory role played by such notions. So perhaps it is necessary to develop alternative means for justifying idealizations (as Davey's contextualism), since some or most idealizations may be indispensable. Last, all this is further complicated by the fact that ascriptions of idealization/de-idealization necessitate inter-pretation of theory and may in turn depend on one's position regarding ontology, fundamentality and scale, modality, induction and confirmation, and so forth.

5 Platonism

In this section, I will connect between the literature on idealization and the debate between mathematical realists/Platonists and anti-realist/nominalists as it arises in the context of indispensability arguments by looking at the case study of fractional quantum statistics.

To start, consider Alan Baker's (2005, 2009) modification of the Putnam–Quine indispensability argument (Putnam 1971; Quine 1981), wherein the

---

[21] Also see discussion of Liu (2019) in Section 6.

emphasis is placed on explanatory indispensability (instead of indispensability tout court), dubbed the Enhanced Indispensability Argument (EIA):

(1) We ought rationally to believe in the existence of any entity that plays an indispensable explanatory role in our best scientific theories.
(2) Mathematical objects play an indispensable explanatory role in science.
(3) Hence, we ought rationally to believe in the existence of mathematical objects.

(Baker 2009, 613)

Many scientific realists base their realism, for example, their belief in the existence of unobservable objects like electrons, in an enhanced indispensability argument applied to unobservable entities. On pain of an unjustified double standard, the EIA implies that said realists ought to be Platonists assuming that there are bona fide examples of mathematical explanation in the sciences (Baker 2009; Colyvan 2001). However, by the same standards, such realists-Platonists ought to rationally believe in the existence of explanatorily indispensable idealizations. In what follows, I first present an example in which idealizations ostensibly play an explanatory role analogous to mathematical objects (based on Shech 2019b) and then consider Platonist attempts to break the symmetry between explanatory idealizations and mathematical explanations (as in Baron 2016, 2019).

Consider a collection of noninteracting, identical particles in thermal equilibrium. What are the possible ways that such a collection may occupy a set of available discrete energy states? Roughly, quantum and statistical mechanics tell us that there are two such ways, and that the expected number of particles in some specific energy state will depend on the type of particle at hand. Bosons manifest a behavior consistent with Bose–Einstein statistics, while fermions distribute themselves according to Fermi–Dirac statistics. This division into particle types, along with the corresponding statistics, may be captured by what is known as the symmetrization/anti-symmetrization postulate: "The states of a system containing N identical particles are necessarily either all symmetrical or all antisymmetrical with respect to permutation of N particles" (Messiah 1962, 595). That is, if a collection of N identical particles is represented by the quantum state $\Psi_{(1,2,...,N)}$ and the same collection with, say, particles 1 and 2 permuted is represented by $\Psi_{(2,1,...,N)}$, then the symmetrization/anti-symmetrization postulate tells us that the states must be related in the following manner:

$$\Psi_{(2,1,...,N)} = e^{i\theta}\Psi_{(1,2,...,N)},$$

where the exchange phase θ can take on a value of $\theta = 0$ for a system of bosons with $e^{i\theta} = +1$ and a symmetric quantum state, or it can take a value $\theta = \pi$ for a system of fermions with $e^{i\theta} = -1$ and an antisymmetric quantum state.

There are two fundamental frameworks for understanding permutation invariance in QM and for grounding the symmetrization/anti-symmetrization postulate and its consequences, namely, that there are two basic types of particles and quantum statistics. These are called the *operator* framework and the *configuration space* framework (Landsman 2016; Shech 2019b). Landsman (2016) has argued that, in dimensions greater than two, both frameworks are equivalent and give equivalent verdicts regarding possible particle types and statistics. However, it turns out that in two dimensions the configuration space framework allows the exchange phase to take on *any* value. This permits the framework to represent bosons and fermions, *as well as* other particles known as "anyons," which are said to exhibit "fractional quantum statistics."

Recall that the manner by which a collection of identical particles occupies energy states will depend on the kind of quantum statistics that such a collection manifests, which in turn depends on the type of particle considered. Particle type is decided by how such a collection behaves under permutation, and this behavior is captured by the value of the exchange phase θ and the corresponding phase factor $e^{i\theta}$. In short, on the configuration space framework, two central theorems (see Shech 2019b) dictate that the phase factor $e^{i\theta}$ is equivalent to the one-dimensional unitary representation γ of the fundamental group π_1 of the configuration space Q of the collection of identical particles, symbolized by $\gamma = e^{i\theta}$.[22] It has been shown that the fundamental groups for the two-dimensional ($d = 2$) and three-dimensional ($d = 3$) cases are given by:

$$\pi_1(Q) = B_N \text{ for } d = 2$$
$$\pi_1(Q) = S_N \text{ for } d = 3,$$

where S_N is the permutation group and B_N is the braid group. In other words, in three dimensions the fundamental group of the configuration space is the (finite and discrete) permutation group S_N, which admits of the known one-dimensional unitary representation: $\gamma = \pm 1$ ($+1$ for bosons and -1 for fermions). In two dimensions, the fundamental group is the (infinite and discrete) braid group B_N with one-dimensional unitary representations giving rise to phase factors of the form: $\gamma_{(\theta)} = e^{i\theta}$ where $0 \leq \theta \leq 2\pi$ so that the exchange

---

[22] Roughly, the "one-dimensional unitary representation" will allow us to represent groups with numbers. The "fundamental group," also known as the first homotopy group, is a topological invariant that allows one to classify topological spaces according to whether paths/loops in the space can be continuously deformed into each other.

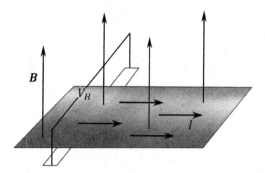

Figure 8 The Hall effect

phase can take on a continuous range of factors allowing for bosons, fermions, and anyons.

But what use is there in fractional statistics? It seems that there are systems that can manifest such behavior. Particularly when a thin current carrying conductor is subjected to a perpendicular magnetic field $B = (0, 0, B)$, there exists a Lorentz force due to the magnetic field acting on the current, which induces an electric field and gives rise to a novel voltage difference dubbed the "Hall voltage" V_H. This is known as the Hall effect, and it was discovered by Edwin Hall in 1879 (see Figure 8). Classically, through Ohm's law $R = V/I$ (where R is the resistance, V voltage difference, and I the electric current) we expect the traverse resistance R_{xy}, also known as the Hall resistance $R_H = V_H/I$, to vary *linearly* with the applied magnetic field according to $R_H = B/eN$ (where e is the electron charge and N is the number of electrons per unit area) and for there to be some *nonvanishing* longitudinal resistance R_{xx}. Contrary to classical expectation, experiments due to von Klitzing and colleagues (1980) and Tsui and colleagues (1982) have shown that (i) the Hall resistance is *quantized* and exhibits plateaus, and that (ii) the longitudinal resistance *vanishes* for values of R_H given by $R_H = h/e^2\nu$ where h is Planck's constant (see Figure 9). The dimensionless number ν – the so-called filling factor, which describes a ratio of filled to vacant electron states – has either integer or fractional values. The former case is known as the integral quantum Hall effect and the latter case is known as the fractional quantum Hall effect (FQHE).[23] What matters most for our purposes is that the mechanism of localization, in the form of quasi-particles that interact with impurities, is appealed to in order to explain (i) in the FQHE. Importantly, it has been argued that *such quasi-particles have fractional quantum statistics and thus are anyons* (Arovas et al. 1984).

---

[23] For more on anyons and the quantum Hall effects, see Bain (2016), Shech (2015b, 2019a, 2019b), and Stern (2008) and references within.

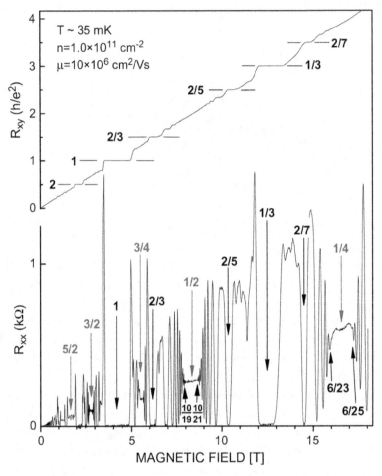

Figure 9 Hall resistance $R_H = R_{xy}$ and longitudinal resistance R_{xx} as a
function of applied magnetic field (from Stern 2008, 207)

In sum, the FQHE is partly explained by the emergence of anyons (particles
obeying fractional quantum statistics) and we want to inquire whether an
idealization plays an indispensable role in such an explanation. The standard
story found in the physics literature is that it is in virtue of the fact that the
fundamental group of the configuration space of identical particles in two
dimensions is the braid group B_N, and not the permutation group S_N, that allows
for the emergence of anyons and fractional statistics. We have to appeal to
abstract mathematical structure in the form of the braid group B_N in order to
explain a physical phenomenon, specifically, fractional statistics as they arise in
physical FQHE systems. Significantly, the said structure is a property of an
idealized two-dimensional system. It is solely in two dimensions that the

fundamental group is the braid group. In three dimensions the structure allowing for fractional statistics disappears. Hence, it seems that the scientific explanation of the FQHE, viz., that (1) the Hall resistance is *quantized* and exhibits plateaus, appeals indispensably to the mathematical-topological properties of an idealization, viz., a two-dimensional system. According to the EIA, then, we ought to rationally commit to the existence of such idealized two-dimensional systems. Since such systems are not concrete – all actual systems are, strictly speaking, three dimensional – their ontological status is likely akin to abstract mathematical entities such as the braid group structure itself.

However, perhaps it is possible to nominalize away ontological commitment to idealized two-dimensional systems by appealing to an approach suggested by Mary Leng (2012). Specifically, Leng is a scientific realist and mathematical nominalist; she thinks we can dispense with reifying explanatory mathematical structure when that structure can both play its explanatory role and is approximately instantiated in nature. Applied to our current example, one could argue that the essential explanatory structure, the braid group, is approximately instantiated in FQHE systems that are approximately (dynamically) two dimensional. However, by appealing to Norton's (2012) distinction between idealization and approximation (see Section 2), I have argued that in the FQHE case the explanatory structure isn't "approximately instantiated" in the manner that Leng's account necessitates (Shech 2019b). The fundamental group of the configuration space of identical particles in approximately two dimensions is the same as that of three dimensions, viz., the permutation group S_N. In order to allow for fractional statistics, we need the fundamental group to be the braid group B_N, and this can only occur in *exactly* two dimensions. Yet physical systems are not exactly two dimensional. Thus, it cannot be said that a physical system "approximately instantiates" the braid group structure necessary for fractional statistics. Nonetheless, on the lack of justificatory grounds discussed in Section 4, one could object that if braid group structure isn't approximately instantiated in real FQHE systems then it cannot explain the real effect. I set this objection aside (but see Shech 2019b for a response) and instead look at two attempts at breaking the ostensible explanatory symmetry between idealizations and mathematical objects, and thus preventing the reification of the former.

In contrast with cases of bona fide mathematical explanation championed by Platonists, Baron (2016) argues that, although idealizations play an indispensable explanatory role in our best sciences, they do not carry the "explanatory load." His idea is that ontological commitment ought to be allocated solely to the indispensable explanatory parts of our scientific explanations that carry the explanatory load, which can further be identified via a difference making account cashed out in terms of counterfactuals (Baron 2016, 372):

> **Explanatory load** A statement S that is (i) about some Fs and (ii) is a part of an explanation E of some phenomenon P is helping to carry the explanatory load iff F makes a difference to P.

> **Difference-making** F makes a difference to P iff had F not been the case, P would not have been the case.

The claim then is that, while some mathematical entities both satisfy the EIA and carry the explanatory load, no indispensable idealizations carry the explanatory load.

Bianchi (2016) criticizes Baron's account in that it presupposes that we can clearly distinguish between idealized objects, properties, systems, models, and so forth, and abstract mathematical (but not idealized) objects, properties, systems, models, and so forth. She argues that our ability to make such distinctions is not well supported by examples from mathematical physics. For instance, in FQHE, it is the *mathematical-topological* braid group structure of an *idealized* two-dimensional system that is carrying the explanatory load and it isn't clear how to differentiate between the mathematical and the idealized parts. Moreover, even if we assume that we can distinguish between an idealized two-dimensional system and the abstract (but non-idealized) topological braid group structure (associated with said system), it still isn't the case that Baron's account succeeds in breaking the explanatory symmetry. Instead, it seems that on the standard explanatory story of anyons in the FQHE one needs *both* the abstract mathematical structure that is the braid group and also the consideration of an idealized two-dimensional system. Within the two-dimensional setting, we can derive the braid group structure which, in turn, allows us to derive fractional quantum statistics. Without the two-dimensional setting, no such derivation seems currently possible.

More recently, Baron (2019, 8) again attempts to break the explanatory symmetry by distinguishing between "constructive" and "substantive" indispensability:

> A claim is constructively indispensable to an explanation when that claim is explanatorily indispensable to our current best scientific theories but there is reason to suppose that the claim can be dispensed with, it is just that we don't know how to do so yet. A claim is substantively indispensable, by contrast, when that claim is explanatorily indispensable to our current best scientific theories and there is no reason to suppose that the claim can be dispensed with.

What grounds the distinction are two senses of impossibility, viz., "it being impossible to explain [phenomenon] P without [claim] C and it being impossible to explain P without C using a particular explanation E." In other words, C may be explanatorily indispensable to P given an "actual explanation" E, but it may be "modally dispensable" if some other "possible explanation" E* of P exists wherein C does not hold. But how do we know if any possible explanations are in the offing?

Setting aside the obvious case in which alternative explanations appear in scientific literature, Baron identifies two such ways: argue that de-idealization is possible – a path we are assuming is blocked in the fractional statistics case (Shech 2019b)[24] – or argue that "coherence" fails. The latter option, which Baron pursues, amounts to an argument that it is "possible to develop a consistent, complete and accurate scientific account of nature." This argument is in part powered by a historical induction:

> [The] history of science bears witness to an impressive application of our epistemic abilities to uncover complex truths about nature ... We have been able to develop consistent, complete and accurate theories of natural phenomena in at least a limited manner to date ... To be sure the generation of theories that unify across more than a restricted class of physical phenomena is a difficult task, but we should not lose sight of the fact that we are very good at producing localised theories. Given that we have the ability to develop such localised theories, and given that we have been able to develop a number of such theories in the past, we have a moderate inductive basis for inferring that the rest of the universe will be more of the same.

In our present context, Baron's (2019) suggestion manifests as a general optimism that we will be able to derive the braid group structure for approximately two-dimensional systems or else offer a different explanation that doesn't appeal to the idealization of two-dimensional systems, while maintaining the essentiality of some mathematical structure. Unfortunately, it is unlikely that such sentiments will convince either those moved by the pessimistic meta-induction or folks who are skeptical of the cogency of historical inductions (e.g., Shech 2019c). Moreover, as noted in Section 4, additional interpretive issues, say, concerning interpretations of quantum theory, make the assessment of coherence exceedingly demanding. In fact, the EIA itself is meant to aid in the project of ontological interpretation so it is difficult to see how Baron can avoid a charge of circulatory. Namely, assessing ontological commitment via the EIA necessitates assessing coherence, but assessing coherence necessitates interpreting the ontological commitments of our best scientific theories, which is what the EIA is supposed to help us in with in the first place!

To end, I would like to consider a worry to the effect that all of this conflates idealized objects like models with mathematical entities.[25] Idealizations are usually model systems, which are cleaned-up real systems, that arise from cases

---

[24] But see Shech (2015b) for a discussion and see Section 4 for more on de-idealization.

[25] Thanks to two anonymous reviewers for raising this point.

in which the systems behind some phenomena of interest are easily recognizable. However, when phenomena are not close to the underlying mechanisms, we have to guess what entities or systems are doing the work, and they are often the result of the imagination. For Platonists, these entities may well be real, but empiricists think that they are fictional characters. Still, even if such entities are literally characterized, we are by no means obligated to believe in their existence and the activity that concerns Platonism is outside the province of idealization.

In reply, consider two points. First, characterizing idealizations as cleaned-up-model systems and distinguishing them from fictions (that are the results of our imagination as described earlier) is an example of a characterization of idealizations narrowly construed. Although I have no doubt that such a distinction may fit many cases of idealizations/fictions in science and may play an important role in arguing for some philosophical thesis, there will be many contexts for which said distinction won't be helpful. For example, the distinction does not fit well with Norton's (2012) construal of idealizations versus approximation, and it is the notion of an approximation that Norton uses to deflate the problem of idealization in the context of PT (discussed further in Section 6). Similarly, while infinitely long and absolutely impenetrably solenoids, truly two-dimensional systems, and infinitely large (in volume and in particle number) kettles all are intuitively idealizations, it is far from clear that these are cleaned-up-model systems. Accordingly, although one can distinguish between an idealization like a truly two-dimensionally FQHE system and a mathematical entity such as the braid group, I don't believe that the only relevant distinction for the idealization literature concerns one of idealizations-as-cleaned-up systems and fictions.

Second, insofar as the EIA is sound, it can be used to reify an entity/system so long as that entity/system plays an indispensable explanatory role in our best sciences. Even though mathematical entities like numbers and idealizations like frictionless planes are, prima facie, different, they can both be reified if it can be argued that both play indispensable explanatory roles and if attempts to break the symmetry between the role that mathematics and idealizations play in science fails. Thus, both are relevant for the Platonist versus nominalist debate.

6 Realism

In Section 5, we showed that an ostensible explanatory symmetry exists between mathematical objects and idealizations, and we considered ways to break such symmetry. In this section, we'll look to the much-discussed paradox of phase transitions to see how said symmetry and paradox may relate to the scientific realism debate.

Scientific realism is, roughly, the view that the entities (including unobservable entities like electrons) postulated by our best scientific theories exist and behave approximately as our theories say they do. There are various dimensions to realism and the doctrine has been characterized in different manners (Chakravartty 2017). For example, the semantic dimension concerns interpreting the claims of scientific theories literally, as ones satisfying truth conditions. There are also prominent anti-realist positions like constructive empiricism that adopt a literal interpretation of theories in regard to claims about observables. The epistemic dimension regards the empirical and explanatory success of science as evidence for the (approximate) truth of the claims of science. That is, often, realists appeal to the idea that the best explanation of the success of science is that our theories are approximately true. But if idealizations are essential to the characterization, representation, explanation, and so forth, of some particular phenomenon, and if one does not want to commit to Platonism about idealized objects, we are left with a kind of paradox in which our theories are true (because of the abductive inference) and not true (because of idealization) (Shech 2013). I'll first illustrate this point in the context of phase transitions (PT) and then continue to discuss some recent attempts at solving the paradox, specifically in relation to scientific realism.

PT concern rapid phenomenological changes occurring to substances or objects, and include a wide array of phenomena such as kettles boiling, iron magnetizing, graphite converting into diamond, and an insulator transitioning to a conductor.[26] Figure 10 is a schematic phase diagram wherein regions corresponding to different possible states or phases of a substance, including solid, liquid, and vapor, are delineated. The bold lines in the figure are known as coexistence lines. Crossing such lines marks transitioning from one phase to another – for example, boiling, freezing, melting – while a point on the line represents a substance that manifests two different phases at once. Point C, the "critical point" corresponding to the "critical temperature" T_c, represents the region of critical phenomena. Below the critical temperature, crossing a coexistence line marks first-order PT and in thermodynamics this corresponds in Figure 11 to a non-analyticity (i.e., a point that is not infinitely differentiable, also known as a "discontinuity," "singularity," or "kink") in the *first* derivative of one of the thermodynamic potentials, such as the Gibbs free energy $G_{TD} = H - TS$ or the Helmoltz free energy $A_{TD} = U - TS$, where H is the

---

[26] The following is based on Shech (2019a). For the theory of phase transitions see Stanley (1971) and Kadanoff (2000).

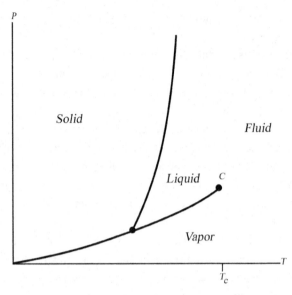

Figure 10 A schematic phase diagram with coexistence lines signified in bold and the critical point C corresponding critical temperature T_c

enthalpy, T temperature, S entropy, and U the internal energy. I'll denote such first-order non-analyticities in G_{TD} and A_{TD}, corresponding to first-order PT, with G_{TD}' and A_{TD}', respectively. Non-analyticities in higher-order derivatives have to do with continuous PT where critical phenomena and universality arises.[27]

Statistical mechanics (SM) follows thermodynamics in representing PT with non-analyticities in the free energies, which I will denote G_{SM} and A_{SM} (with G_{SM}' and A_{SM}' for the first-order non-analytic cases). That said, G_{SM} and A_{SM} are expressed as functions of a partition function Z, $G(Z)$ and $A(Z)$. A partition function is an expression that contains information about the various micro-states (along with their probabilities) available to a system: $Z = \sum_s e^{-\beta H(s)}$, where $\beta = 1/k_B T$ is the inverse temperature T, k_B the Boltzmann constant, and $H(s)$ the Hamiltonian (or energy) associated with a microstate s. In Gibbsian SM, the probability $P(s)$ of a system being in microstate s is given by $P(s) = e^{-\beta H(s)}/Z$.

Crucial for our purposes, the partition function is a sum of analytic functions $\sum_s e^{-\beta H(s)}$, but any such finite sum cannot display a non-analyticity. In order to avoid this result, one must take the thermodynamic limit (TDL) in which the particle number N diverges (while other constraints are obeyed, e.g., the density

---

[27] See the brief discussion of universality in Section 4.

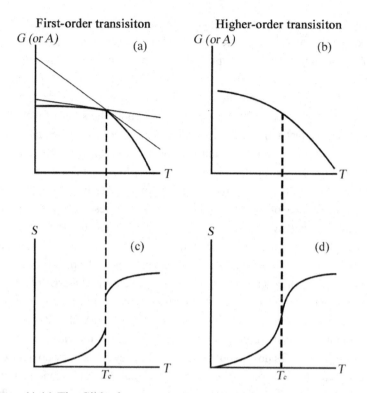

Figure 11 (a) The Gibbs free energy G_{TD} or the Helmholtz free energy A_{TD} portraying a first-order phase transitions, corresponding to (c) a discontinuity in the entropy S, and (b) higher-order (continuous) phase transitions with (d) a corresponding non-discontinuous entropy S (instead, the discontinuity appears in the in the heat capacity). $S = -\left(\dfrac{\partial G}{\partial T}\right)_P$ or $-\left(\dfrac{\partial A}{\partial T}\right)_V$ (from Stanley 1971, 32)

$\dfrac{N}{V}$ remains constant as $V \to \infty$). As an illustration, notice that the series $\sum_{n=0}^{N} x^n = 1 + x + x^2 + \ldots + x^N$ has no non-analyticity for any finite sum. But if we allow for infinite sum in which $N \to \infty$, the series tends toward $\dfrac{1}{1-x}$ and has a non-analyticity at $x = 1$. We need to take the limit in order to get the non-analyticity. Likewise, we need to take the TDL in order to allow for non-analytic partition functions to arise, along with corresponding non-analytic free energies:

$$\lim_{N \to \infty} G(Z) = G_{SM}' = G_{TD}' \ \& \ \lim_{N \to \infty} A(Z) = A_{SM}' = A_{TD}'.$$

It is for this reason that authoritative physicists have claimed that PT, strictly speaking, only arises in infinite systems: "The existence of a phase transition requires an infinite system. No phase transitions occur in systems with a finite number of degrees of freedom" (Kadanoff 2000, 238). Also, "The physical systems to which the thermodynamic formalism applies are idealized to be actually infinite" (Ruelle 2004, 2). Naturally, philosophers have followed suit: "A well-known fact about phase transitions is that even though they take place in finite systems, they can be accounted for only by invoking the thermodynamic limit [and] this happens only in infinite systems" (Morrison 2012, 156–158).

It is worthwhile to note that by "finite" systems we mean systems represented with "finite degrees of freedom," which generally corresponds to a corpuscular ontology associated with the atomistic theory of matter; by "infinite" systems we mean systems represented with "infinite degrees of freedom," which generally corresponds to a continuous or field-like ontology. The paradox of PT then ostensibly arises once a realist attitude is taken to our best theories of PT, either because one interprets the theoretical representation of PT literally, or because one argues via an indispensability argument (like the EIA) that PTs as characterized in infinite systems play an ontologically committing indispensable role. The result is that PTs do and do not exist in finite systems: they do not exist in finite systems because our best theories tell us that PTs can't manifest in finite systems; they do exist in finite systems because our world abounds with (finite) boiling kettles.

Before continuing to discuss ostensible solutions to the paradox, it is worthwhile to note that there are different paths to generating the paradox and these will depend on one's specific commitment to realism. For example, if you are a scientific realist about unobservables but a mathematical nominalist about abstracta, who is further moved by indispensability arguments like the EIA, then the paradox will arise if one can show that idealizations are explanatorily indispensable for some phenomenon (such as the case of idealized two-dimensional systems and the FQHE in Section 5). The reason is that you will be committed to existence of abstracta via the EIA applied to idealizations, but you will also be committed to the nonexistence of abstracta due to your nominalism. Moreover, even a constructive empiricist/anti-realist who commits to interpreting theories literately and believing that theoretical claims regarding observables are true (while maintaining that claims about unobservables are only empirically adequate) must contend with the paradox. Again, this is because our best theories about observable PT allegedly tell us that they can only occur in infinite systems.[28]

---

[28] Of course, an anti-realist could attempt to evade the paradox by denying that there are particles, but likely they wouldn't deny that systems are finite volume.

In order to connect with suggested resolutions, we will generalize the paradox of PT in three steps. First, following Butterfield (2011) and Norton (2012), we distinguish between a system S_N and some property of S_N, which we represent with a function $f_N := f_{S_N}$. Consider a sequence of such systems $\{S_1, S_2, \ldots, S_N\}$ and corresponding functions $\{f_1, f_2, \ldots, f_N\}$ (where N is a natural number) when one takes the infinite limit $N \to \infty$. It is important to note that there is a difference between a property of a well-defined infinite systems called the "limit system" (Norton 2012, 212), viz., "what is true at that limit" (Butterfield 2011, 1075), on one hand, and the corresponding "limit property" (Norton 2012, 212) that is "the limit of a sequence of functions" (Butterfield 2011, 1075), on the other. Specifically, a "limit property" has to do with (i) the limit f_∞ of the sequence $\{f_1, f_2, \ldots, f_N\}$ of functions and a property of a "limit system" corresponds to (ii) the function f_{S_∞} associated with the limit system S_∞. Recall Norton's (2012) distinction between idealization and approximation (Section 2) and consider some target system. The limit property (f_∞) is an approximation – that is, an inexact description of some property of the target – while the limit system (S_∞) is an idealization, some of whose properties (f_{S_∞}) may provide inexact descriptions of some properties of the target system.

Second, Palacios and Valente (2021, 322; original emphasis) claim that the following three propositions give rise to the "Paradox of Infinite Limits:"

(I)' *Finiteness of Real Systems*: If S_N represents a real system, then the variable [N] corresponding to some physical parameter cannot take on infinite values.

(II)' *Indispensability of the Limit System*: The explanation of the phenomenon P can *only* be given by means of claims about a limit system S_∞ constructed in the limit [$N \to \infty$].

(III)' *Enhanced Indispensability Argument (EIA)*: If a claim plays an indispensable role in the explanation of P we ought to believe its existence.

They maintain that (I)' is "a basic desideratum of scientific realism," since "according to our most successful theories, such as the atomic theory of matter" systems are generally finite (323). (II)' is a supposed fact about our current science and (III)' is also motivated by realism.

However, it does not follow from the atomic theory of matter that we must *represent* real target systems realistically and insofar as realistic representation is necessitated by realism, (I)' is superfluous. Moreover, as noted earlier, depending on one's realist attitude, the EIA may not be necessary for generating the paradox. Relatedly, depending on one's realist attitude, it isn't clear that (II)' ought to be stated in strong modal terms (as discussed in Sections 4 and 5). Last, regarding (III)', the EIA doesn't not imply that we believe in the existence of claims or even interpret claims (say) about S_∞ literally. Rather, if it can be shown that S_∞ plays an indispensable explanatory role, then the EIA entails that S_∞ exists. However, even though this may imply a kind of Platonism (as discussed in Section 5) since S_∞ is naturally construed as abstract, no paradox arises. Instead, it follows both that P exists by stipulation and that S_∞ exists. In the case of PT, the "point is that without adding additional tenets that make a claim about the relation between, on the one hand, concrete PT occurring in physical systems and, on the other hand, the abstract mathematical [or theoretical] representation of concrete PT, which arise in scientific accounts of PT, no paradox arises" (Shech 2013, 1173).

Instead, as a third step, I'd suggest the following reconstruction (based on Shech 2013) of the paradox. Namely, let P be a phenomenon in the world, which is the object of scientific inquiry, with some property or attribute A associated with P, such as P occurring in finite systems and being concrete. Consider propositions (I)–(III):

(I) *Real systems*: Based on normal perceptions, background beliefs, and/or our best scientific theories, we take P to exist in the world and to have property/attribute A.

(II) *Idealization in science*: Our best scientific account of phenomenon P is given by means of claims about an idealized system S_∞ (which may be a limit system constructed in the limit $N \to \infty$), with associated property/attribute A_∞ (where $A_\infty \neq A$).

(III) *Realism*: Some realist attitude (e.g., commitment to some indispensability argument like the EIA or a literal interpretation of theories) entails that we *impute A_∞ to P*.

(I) implies that P has A, (II) and (III) imply that P has A_∞, but $A_\infty \neq A$ so a paradox arises: P has and does not have A. Again, depending on the details – for example, whether an idealization arises in the theoretical-scientific character-ization of P, or in its explanation – various realist attitudes can engender the paradox and the EIA is just a special case in which an idealization is explana-torily indispensable. What is key to engendering the paradox is that one has good reasons to impute contradictory properties/attributes to some target phe-nomenon or system. This is a somewhat different issue from the question of whether one's realist commitments ought to be extended given the roles that idealizations play in science. As noted earlier, even an anti-realist (about both unobservables and abstracta) may have to contend with the paradox if P is observable (as in the case of PT), if indeed idealizations are indispensable to our best scientific accounts of P, and if said anti-realist is committed to a literal interpretation of scientific theories.

Next, recalling that (i) concerns a limit property and (ii) a property of a limit system, a presentation of ostensible solutions to the paradox engendered by (I)–(III) is aided with a four-fold taxonomy of infinite limits (Palacios and Valente 2021, 322):

1. *Approximations without idealizations*, where (ii) is not well defined [so no limit system exists], or (i) is empirically correct but (ii) is not;
2. *Idealizations yielding approximations*, where (i) and (ii) are well defined and equal; and
3. *Essential idealizations*, where (i) and (ii) are well defined but are not equal, and (ii) rather than (i) is empirically correct.
4. *Abstractions*, where (i) and (ii) are well defined and we reinterpret S_∞ as a minimalist idealization/minimal model.[29]

Several options are open to dissolving the (infinite) idealization paradox entailed by (I)–(III). One can reject (I) and conclude that contrary to our beliefs, science teaches us that P doesn't have attribute A. For instance, one may suggest that there is a sense in which systems undergoing PT are not actually finite either because the ontology associated with the "true" governing theory involves an infinite number of degrees of freedom (e.g., as in fields in QFT); or else such systems may be coupled to external systems: "Assuming that the correct description of a boiling kettle requires infinitely many degrees of freedom, it is reasonable to say that, since the kettle contains finitely many atoms, and so finitely many mechanical degrees of freedom, other degrees of freedom – e.g. of the electromagnetic field – must somehow be involved" (Butterfield 2011, 1078).

Alternatively, one could dissolve the tension that arises by imputing both A_∞ and A to P by appealing to the notion of scale relative ontology (Ladyman and Ross 2007; Shech and McGivern 2021), or the distinction between data and phenomena (Bangu 2019). In the former case, the idea is that while, relative to some higher-level scale P has A_∞, relative to some lower-level scale P has A. For example, while the fundamental ontology associated with FQHE systems concerns field excitations, at the high-level low-energy scale FQHE are really composed of quasi-particles (that perhaps obey fractional statistics). In the latter case, we say that P-qua-data has A but that P-qua-phenomenon has A_∞. For instance, Bangu (2019, 16) distinguishes "between phase transitions considered at the observational, or data level, on one hand, and phase transitions understood as phenomena on the other" and he "claims that singularities are referential in this latter sense." Another option is to reject (II) by identifying good reasons to be optimistic about alternative *scientific* accounts of P that do not involve

---

[29] Compare Sections 2 and 3.

idealization. Such an approach is exemplified by Menon and Callender (2013), Ardourel (2018), and Baron (2019) in the context of PT and by Shech (2015b) in the case of fractional statistics.

Several additional options concern the rejection of (III). On the extreme end, we can abandon the realist attitude that commits us to imputing A_∞ to P. Depending on the details, one could embrace an instrumentalism that doesn't interpret theories literally, reject indispensability arguments, try to break the symmetry between idealizations and those entities that one is happy to commit to via indispensability arguments (Baron 2016; Leng 2012), or else adopt an alternative form of realism that dissolves the paradox. For example, Liu (2019, 29) argues for a kind of "contextual realism," where "realist claims about any types of disputed objects can only be evaluated as true or false within a context, and a context is determined or defined by its anchoring assumptions." Anchoring assumptions serve to "insulate parts or levels of reality" and "the *anchoring* or *grounding* assumption that defines the context of [the PT] case is that *condensed matter is continuous*" (25; original emphasis). In other words, relative to the context in which condensed matter is *continuous*, a boiling kettle has an infinite number of degrees of freedom, while relative to the microscopic context, a boiling kettle has a finite number of degrees of freedom associated with its finite atomistic nature. More generally, relative to one context P has A_∞, relative to another context P has A, so no paradox arises.

From a semantic perspective, Liu's (2019) account is similar to Davey's (2011) contextualism discussed in Section 4, in which truth conditions for propositions are always decided relative to a set of standards. Both accounts stress that science itself plays a role in deciding on the appropriate anchoring assumptions or standards relative to which truth assignments are assessed. From a metaphysical perspective, however, Liu's (2019, 29) contextualism places an emphasis on how it is "a feature of reality itself that makes the anchoring assumptions possible" (29). This suggests that the view is similar to, or at least complemented by, the idea of scale relative ontology noted earlier. For instance, following Batterman's (2006) distinction between ontological and epistemological fundamentality, Shech and McGivern (2021) suggest that the examples of PT and of anyons in the FQHE both support their motto of "ontology being scale dependent":

> If electrons are the only things that are real in [fractional quantum Hall] systems, it is not clear how the FQHE can be explained. Instead, if being real is being real on some scale, then both electrons and quasi-particles (and their properties and behaviors) can be real. It then makes sense to appeal to entities and behaviors prominent in the low-energy scale in order to explain low-energy effects such as the FQHE. Similarly, connecting with the phase

transition example, phase transitions are macroscopic phenomena since it makes no sense to talk about a phase transition of one or two molecules. Thus, it is not surprising that statistical mechanics (a microscale theory) needs to appeal to the thermodynamic limit (the region of macroscopic thermodynamics) in order to explain a macroscopic phenomenon. (1425)

[The] higher-level macroscopic theory representing a system undergoing a phase transition is thermodynamics, and it models systems like boiling water in a kettle as a continuous fluid – it is indifferent to molecular structure. The lower-level microscopic theory is statistical mechanics and it represents such systems as a collection of particles ... In taking the thermodynamic limit, it is suggested that we are in essence transitioning from the (ontologically fundamental) microscopic scale and realm of finite number of degrees of freedom, i.e., the regime of statistical mechanics proper, to the (perhaps epistemologically fundamental) macroscopic scale and realm of an infinite number of degrees of freedom, i.e., the regime of thermodynamics. (1413–1414)

Another, more moderate, option is to argue that our realist attitudes notwithstanding, we aren't committed to imputing A_∞ to P. First, this may be because the idealizations associated with P are either idealizations-yielding approximations, in which case they can be demoted to approximations, or else they were approximations without idealizations all along (Norton 2012). Such an approach may be bolstered by an additional alternative *philosophical interpretation* of given scientific accounts of P, which basically speaks in favor of in-principle de-idealization that blocks imputing A_∞ to P. For instance, Butterfield (2011) suggests the following characterization for PT in finite systems: "phase transitions occur in the finite system iff [G_{SM}' or A_{SM}'] has non-analyticities." The justification for appealing to properties of an idealized limit system (viz., G_{SM}' or A_{SM}') in characterizing finite PT is given through an identification that the idealizations involved either yield approximations or were approximation all along. In the case of first-order PT, Palacios and Valente (2021) generalize Butterfield's solution to cases of ostensible essential idealization. The idea is that "empirically correct results can be approximately obtained already on the way to the limit for the relevant physical quantities [represented by $\{f_1, f_2, \ldots, f_N\}$] of interest." To my mind, this is just another way to argue that the idealization involved in characterizing first-order PT is, in fact, not essential to the representation of physical PT in the world.

Second, it may be possible to reinterpret the idealization as a case of abstraction, in which S_∞ is understood as a kind of minimalist idealization/ minimal model that abstracts away all details that aren't difference-makers for P. Thus, one's realist attitudes no longer vindicate *imputing A_∞* to P, and so no paradox arises. For instance, the TDL allows one to remove contributions to the partition function that come from the system's edge/boundary (Butterfield 2011), and, insofar as this is its main role in a particular characterization and/or explanation of PT, one can reinterpret the idealized limit system S_∞ as an abstract minimal model that is partially true of the target (Jones 2006). Palacios and Valente (2021) suggest that this is part of the way to handle the ostensible essential idealizations that arise in RG explanations of critical phenomena like continuous PT. This idea is partly justified by the fact that RG explanations appeal to an infinite limit of RG iterations. But in each RG iteration "irrelevant coupling constant are abstracted away" (344) and the "number of iterations is not a physical parameter" (346), so it is reasonable to interpret the limit of infinite RG iterations as an abstraction. Renormalization group explanations also appeal to the idealized TDL limit, but Palacios (2019) and Wu (2021) suggest ways to demote said idealization to an approximation. It is controversial, though, whether the idealizations involved in RG explanations can truly be de-idealized or reinterpreted as abstraction, as some seem to maintain that they cannot (Batterman 2002; Batterman and Rice 2014; Morrison 2015).

Last, one could argue that the idealized description S_∞ contains *true and accurate modal* information about P (Earman 2019; Rice 2021; Saatsi 2016; Shech 2018a, 2018b, 2022a). The idea is to block imputing A_∞ to P by holding that A_∞ is relevant for a *possible P* that is faithfully represented by S_∞. In Section 1, for example, we discussed how the idealizations I1–I3 in the AB effect facilitate exploring the modal structure of QM. Here we're thinking of S_∞ as the abstract AB effect with the property/attribute A_∞ that the magnetic field is completely shielded (as with I1–I3), while P concerns the concrete AB effect as it is manifested in the laboratory with the property/attribute A that the magnetic field is *approximately* completely shielded (so that I1–I3 are partially de-idealized). While one may be hard-pressed to explain the presence of the *actual* AB effect by appealing to the *possible* but idealized effect, it may be the case that the latter sheds light on quantum theory and in doing so helps us indirectly better understand the nature of the former. More generally, if an idealization is indispensable for understanding the modal structure of a theory and its phenomena (and thus indirectly essential for understanding actual phenomena governed by said theory), but can, in principle, be de-idealized for the purpose of deriving an actual P from theory, then we can have our cake and eat it too, so to speak. In principle, de-idealization solves the paradox and offers justification for making use of said idealization. But one can still claim that idealization is essential for providing the sought-after modal information. In the following section we'll explore this idea.

7 Understanding

Science affords understanding of how things work. Why does the temperature of a gas, which is kept at a constant volume in a rigid box, rise when pressure is exerted? Here's a (supposedly) true explanation that presumably produces no understanding. Given the initial conditions of the universe and the universal wave function, it follows from the Schrödinger equation (or its eventual quantum gravity counterpart) that everything is as it is, and so the temperature of said gas rises with pressure by such nomological necessity (albeit, depending on one's favorite interpretation of quantum theory, there may some feature of indeterminacy that will be added to said explanation). While perhaps true, such explanations miss the mark in terms of producing the sought-after understanding. Instead, appeals to the highly idealized, hence false, ideal gas law and its derivation will likely play a greater role in affording understanding of why the temperature rises upon the exertion of pressure in this example.

In the epistemology and philosophy of science literature there has been some debate regarding the role of idealization in affording understanding. Non-factivists (e.g., Doyle et al. 2019; Elgin 2017; Potochnik 2017) hold that false idealized statements produce understanding, while quasi-factivists (e.g., Sullivan and Khalifa 2019) object. Many emphasize that understanding is a key epistemic value provided by idealization (Batterman 2002; Bokulich 2008; de Regt 2017; Rohwer and Rice 2013; Strevens 2008, 2013, 2017) but some claim that only non-epistemic value is involved (Sullivan and Khalifa 2019).

My goal is this section is to gesture at such issues in the context of the AB effect case study (Section 1). I begin by presenting two families of distinctions found in the understanding literature, as well as outlining my own notion of "understanding-what" (Shech 2022a). Then I will discuss how idealizations facilitate understanding in the AB effect by making use of said distinctions. Next, I'll sketch the factivism/non-factivism debate in relation to the AB effect. Note that I follow the norm of using "p," "q," or "P" to symbolize either a phenomenon or scenario/state of affairs, or else a proposition describing a phenomenon, scenario, and so forth (wherein appropriate use can be extrapolated from context). Also, I will distinguish between the target of understanding and the vehicle of understanding – that is, the thing that provides understanding of the target. For a detailed analysis, please see Shech (2022a).

To begin, Strevens (2013) distinguishes between "understanding-why" and "understanding-with." Understanding-why concerns having understanding of why some phenomenon occurs, for example, understanding why p may be constituted by knowing the explanation for p (Bokulich 2008; Khalifa 2017; Strevens 2013). Understanding-with concerns understanding a scientific theory.

For instance, on Strevens's (2013) account, to understand a theory is to be able to use the theory to explain a range of phenomena. Next, many distinguish between explanatory understanding and objectual understanding (e.g., see Stuart 2018 and references within). Explanatory understanding concerns having an explanation for why p and, for accounts of understanding-why that stress the centrality of scientific explanation (Bokulich 2008; de Regt 2017; Khalifa 2017), the two notions overlap.

Objectual understanding has to do with understanding a thing or a domain of things, broadly construed, so that one can grasp and express the relations among events, objects, domains, and so forth, in an appropriate manner. There is some disagreement as to the nature of objectual understanding and its target. Some folks take objectual understanding to concern understanding a topic or subject matter like physics (Elgin 2017), while others (e.g., Newman 2017) take objectual understanding to mean understanding a theory like QM so that the notion overlaps with Strevens's (2013) understanding-with. Still, others take objectual understanding to mean understanding a phenomenon or thing (while resisting reduction to explanatory understanding or understanding-why) (Kelp 2015).

Interestingly, the notions of objectual understanding of a theory (understanding-with) and objectual understanding of a phenomenon can come apart. One can, for example, have an understanding of Newton's gravitational theory and yet not really understand gravity because Newton's theory (where gravity is a force) has been superseded by Einstein's (where gravity is the curvature of spacetime). However, it is crucial to notice that having objectual understanding of certain types of phenomena is strongly entangled with the manner by which the same phenomena are characterized by their governing theory (quantum entangled being a case in point). Since this is the type of objectual understanding of phenomenon that I'm interested in, I'll introduce the term "understanding-what" – as in, understanding what something is *in the first place* – to signify this point.

With these distinctions in mind, and given the analysis of the AB effect and distinctions found in Section 1 (recall Table 1), I'd like to consider how idealizations facilitate understanding-with (a kind of objectual understanding of theory) and understanding-what (a kind of objectual understanding of phenomenon). The basic idea is summed up as follows. Scientific understanding ought to track scientific practice, and the AB effect case study shows that there are possible (but non-actual) worlds according to QM, which are most naturally construed as idealizations (because of I1–I3), and are essential for both understanding-with QM and understanding-what the AB effect is in the first place (Shech 2022a).

Starting with understanding-with, reflection on the AB effect controversy suggests that three factors are indicative of understanding-with, including (but not limited to) (1) knowing a theory's modal structure, (2) knowing a theory's foundations (e.g., is the theory deterministic/indeterministic, local/nonlocal?), and (3) knowing the (relevant) intertheoretical relations (of said theory). As for (3), the language used by proponents of the AB effect controversy suggests an important contrast class, namely, how QM relates to predecessor and competing theories. For instance, Aharonov and Bohm (1959, 490) note that "In classical mechanics ... the potentials have been regarded as purely mathematical auxiliaries, while only the [electromagnetic] field quantities were thought to have a direct physical meaning." They then continue to contrast the classical situation with what they have argued happens in quantum mechanics, viz., the abstract AB effect is predicted. Indeed, the abstract AB effect makes salient the radically different structure of quantum and classical mechanics, via their predictions about the behavior of an electron beam in the vicinity of a *completely* shielded magnetic field. Alternatively, if we de-idealize so that the magnetic field can interact directly with the electron beam, then *both* quantum and classical physics predict shifts in interference pattern.

Moving on to (2), foundational issues arise in the discussion of inter-theoretic relations through both the controversy surrounding the ontological implications of the effect vis-à-vis its causal-mechanistic basis, and the discussion of the meaning gauges and gauge transformations in quantum theory. An example is exhibited by the Healey–Maudlin debate (Healey 1997, 1999; Maudlin 1998) regarding the foundational implications of the abstract AB effect for quantum theory. Healey (1997) argues that there is an interesting analogy between the nonlocality in the abstract AB effect and quantum entanglement: "Neither effect can be given a completely local explanation. But in both cases one may analyze the residual nonlocality as involving the violation either of a principle of local action, or of a principle of separability, or of both" (Healey 1997, 39). In response, Maudlin (1998, 362–363) rejects the foundational import that Healey extracts from said analogy, arguing that the AB effect can be given a local explanation that violates neither local action nor separability. Instead, he suggested that the AB effect "points us to the very important problem of *understanding* the physical significance of quantities which admit of local gauge transformations, indeed of *understanding the meaning* of gauges and gauge transformations *at all*" (Maudlin 1998, 367; my emphasis). Note the role that the abstract AB effect is playing in this debate, namely shedding light on foundational issues concerning quantum mechanics having to do with the nature of locality/nonlocality and gauge transformations – it facilitates understanding quantum theory itself and thus fosters understanding-with.

Finally, it is by exploring (1) the modal structure of quantum mechanics, particularly what it says about possible worlds that are most naturally construed as idealizations (vis-à-vis the abstract AB effects), that we facilitate (2) and (3). Accordingly, I have argued that the AB effect case study suggests the following outline of a modal account of understanding-with (in the spirit of Levy 2020 and Le Bihan 2017):

> Subject S has understanding of a theory T to the extent that S is able to (i) draw accurate and general inferences about phenomena governed by T and navigate the modal space associated with T (i.e., associated with the possible worlds according to T), (ii) answer various foundational questions about T (such as whether T is deterministic/indeterministic, local/non-local, [...] etc.), (iii) elucidate the relations of T to predecessor and competing theories and interpretations.[30] (Shech 2022a, 17)

Next, consider the notion of understanding-what. Part of the historical controversy surrounding the AB effect, its foundational implications, and its experimental verification, had to do with the fact that it was not always clear what the AB effect what supposed to be in the first place. For example, Strocchi and Wightman (1974, 2202), questioned the nature, reality, and confirmation of the AB effect in light of the idealizations (I1–I3) involved: "How then can one understand the Aharonov–Bohm paradoxes? ... The explanation is that the description of Aharonov and Bohm is over-idealized at a decisive point ... The solution of the Schrödinger equation always has a tail which runs into the region of a nonvanishing [magnetic] field and that field, by purely local, manifestly gauge-invariant action produces the effect."

Similarly, in their paper titled "Nonexistence of the Aharonov–Bohm Effect," Bocchieri and Loinger (1978, 475) argued that the AB effect has a "purely mathematical origin" and that their analyses "leave no room for the effects of the kind of Aharonov's and Bohm's" (478). Issues such as whether "there [is] an AB effect if the infinite solenoid is – as AB assume – absolutely impenetrable" were at the front and center of the debate (Bocchieri and Loinger 1981, 168). For instance, Bocchieri and Loinger (1981, 168) argued that:

> If the solenoid is turned on first, and a finite potential barrier is subsequently allowed to become infinite, an AB effect will be observed. [But the effect arises] from the penetration of the particle into the region in which [the

---

[30] One may of course worry that the foregoing account of understanding-with is overly influenced by cases in QM like the AB effect. Admittedly, said account is motivated by cases in QM and thus additional work is needed to test whether the account is generalizable. Still, even if the account is not generalizable it may be important for comprehending how we understanding, say, QM specifically. Given the centrality of QM to our best sciences, it is vital that an account of understanding-with do justice to this point.

magnetic field is nonzero] during the time in which the potential barrier is still finite. [On the other hand, if] one were to imagine that an impenetrable barrier had somehow erected first, and that the solenoid was turned on later, no AB effect would be observed.

Notice in particular that the dispute has to do with what QM predicts about two different *idealized*, counterfactual scenarios.

More generally, if the AB effect was predicted in 1959 and subsequent experimental testing began with Chambers (1960), why is it that the physics community didn't come to accept the effect as a bona fide physical effect until the experiments of Tonomura and colleagues (1986)? Earman (2019) argues that (at least part of) the answer has to do with the fact that the abstract AB effect cannot ever be manifested in the actual world. This leads us to the following puzzle:

> [H]ow can experiments on actual systems serve to confirm the predictions of the theory for the behavior of the fictional system? What conditions must an actual world apparatus satisfy in order that it can produce confirmation of the AB predictions for the fictional apparatus? (Earman 2019, 1992, 2010)

It is worthwhile to pause and consider how odd the situation is. The issue is not about whether experiments can confirm an interference shift due to a magnetic field – they can, and even classically we expect such a shift. Rather, the issue concerns which *actual* experiments can confirm predictions of quantum theory about an *idealized possible* scenario (as in I1–I3), viz., the abstract AB effect.

Historically, Aharonov and Bohm (1959) characterized the AB effect along the lines of what I have been calling the abstract AB effect and discussion of the effect in much of the literature and textbooks uses this conventional definition (focusing on the narrow-abstract AB effect). Aharonov and Bohm also suggested that there is a physical, empirically confirmable manifestation of the effect, viz., the concrete AB effect. Hence, taking the lead from convention, one could characterize the concrete AB effect as the physical counterpart of the abstract AB effect, viz., what we expect to observe in the laboratory (given various rigorous results, e.g., de Oliveir and Pereira 2008, 2010, 2011; Ballesteros and Weder 2009, 2011) when we de-idealize from I1–I3. In this sense, reference to the abstract-narrow AB effect is important if not essential for understanding-what the concrete-narrow AB effect is. But, one may wonder, is it truly necessary? What is the problem of characterizing the AB effect as a concrete, physical phenomenon, eschewing any reference to the idealized, abstract AB effect? Let me discuss first the narrow AB effect and then broad AB effect.

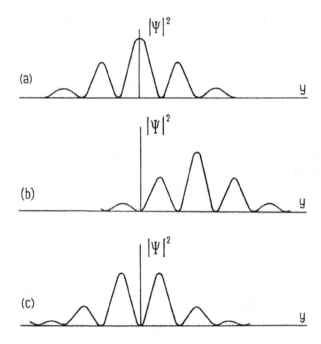

Figure 12 Represents the electronic inference patterns in a double-slit
experiment in three cases: (a) no magnetic field (corresponding to the normal
interference patterns), (b) magnetic field in contact with electrons
(corresponding to an interference shift predicted classically), and (c) shielded
magnetic field that is not in contact with electrons (corresponding to the abstract
AB effect) (from Olariu and Popescu 1985, 51)

One problem with characterizing the concrete-narrow AB effect as shift in
interference pattern due to a *partly* shielded magnetic field is that, classically,
we expect some kind of shift due to the (classical) interaction between the
electron beam and magnetic field. There is nothing novel or surprising about
this type of effect. Still, quantitatively, the predicted shift between the classical
and quantum case will differ slightly (see Figure 12). However, characterized in
this manner, the difference isn't a categorical and qualitative one as the historical controversy suggests, it is just one of degree.

This motivates the following qualification: a shift in interference pattern due
to a partly shielded magnetic field that cannot be explained non-quantum
mechanically (e.g., classically, relativistically). In other words, the effect must
be a genuine, independent quantum effect. However, arguably, any shift in
interference pattern due to an almost shielded magnetic field can be explained
(away) classically. This is part of what led to the 30-year controversy

surrounding the AB effect, and it sustains the debate among some to this day (e.g., Boyer 2000). Consider Tonomura and colleagues (1986, 794) on the matter:

> The most controversial point in the dispute over experimental evidence for the AB effect has been whether or not the [interference] shift would be observed when both electron intensity and magnetic field were extremely small in the region of overlap. Since experimental realization of absolutely zero field is impossible, the continuity of physical phenomena in the transition from negligibly small field to zero field should be accepted instead of perpetual demands for the ideal; if a discontinuity there is asserted, only a futile agnosticism results.

In order to bolster this last claim, consider the context of the concrete-broad AB effect where there is something like an in-principle argument that can be given for why reference to the abstract-broad AB effect is necessary for understanding-what.

Recall that the emergence of the abstract-broad AB effect comes about from the fact that there are different formal implementations of I1–I3, corresponding to different boundary conditions obtained at the solenoid border (viz., Dirichlet, Neumann, Robin), which in turn correspond to different predicted dynamics in (say) scattering experiments. We can then characterize the concrete-broad AB effect as the physical counterpart of the abstract-broad AB effect, viz., what we expect to observe in the laboratory when we de-idealize a bit from I1–I3 given the work of, for example, de Oliveira and Pereira (2010) (see Figure 3).

That said, from a theoretical perspective, once we de-idealize from I1–I3, there is no longer an issue of formally implementing I1–I3. If we transition to the concrete setting where the beam of electrons can access the entire configuration space of $\mathbb{R}^3$, then the natural (initial) domain for Aharonov-Bohm Hamiltonian H^{A_∞} is $D(H^{A_\infty}) = C_0^\infty(\mathbb{R}^3)$ which is dense in $\mathcal{H} = L^2(\mathbb{R}^3)$. With this choice of domain, H^{A_∞} is essentially self-adjoint and there is no need for self-adjoint extensions corresponding to different boundary conditions. In other words, understanding-what the concrete-broad AB effect is in the first place, even more so that the concrete-narrow effect, seems to require an appeal to idealizations in the form of the abstract-broad AB effect. In sum, idealizations in the AB effect afford – and may be necessary for – understanding-with and understanding-what. This concludes our brief discussion of how idealizations facilitate understanding in the AB effect, but see Shech 2022a for further details.

Moving on, does the case study support factivism/non-factivism about understanding? For propositions (or a set of propositions) p and q referring to the target and vehicle of understanding, respectively,[31] Doyle and colleagues (2019, 346) characterize *non-factivism* as the existence of some p and q such that:

(1) p is false;
(2) p provides understanding of q; and
(3) the understanding of q resulting from either not accepting p or accepting a more accurate proposition instead of p is not better than the understanding provided by accepting p.

They call (1)–(3) the *Falsehood Condition*, the *Provision Condition*, and the *Parity Condition*, respectively. For all p and q, if p provides understanding of q, they characterize *quasi-factivism* as follows (347):

(i) p is true; or
(ii) the understanding of q resulting from either not accepting p or accepting a more accurate proposition instead of p is better than the understanding provided by accepting p.

Given these characterizations, Doyle and colleagues (2019) derive the ideal gas law as the equation of state governing a system by starting with the partition function (see Section 6) and assuming that the system consists of identical noninteracting particles. They argue that understanding the ideal gas law is afforded by the assumption of noninteracting particles, since this assumption allows for the derivation of the law while satisfying four cognitive goods: easing calculation (e.g., compared to a de-idealized viral expansion), highlighting irrelevancies (e.g., of particle interaction), facilitating explanation (through derivation), and guiding the construction of new models (viz., through the novel prediction that liquid helium will transition to a Bose condensate at 3.3 K). In doing so, Doyle and colleagues (2019) defend non-factivism.

By the same lights, deriving the abstract AB effect using false assumptions I1–I3 also provides similar cognitive goods, and so this understanding of the abstract AB effect supports non-factivism. But such non-factivism seems trivial: of course, understanding idealized targets (like the abstract AB effect or the ideal gas law) may be afforded by and perhaps necessitates idealizations. The interesting question is whether non-factivism is supported in the context of understanding a physical phenomenon like the concrete AB effect. However, it isn't clear whether the parity condition is satisfied if our target concerns the occurrence of the concrete AB effect and our vehicle is the abstract AB effect. On one hand, de-idealization connects between the abstract and concrete AB

---

effects, so this seems to support quasi-factivism. On the other hand, the abstract AB effect may be essential for understanding-what the concrete AB effect is in the first place and for understanding QM. Perhaps then non-factivism is supported insofar as understanding-why the concrete AB effect occurs is enhanced or presupposes the concepts of understanding-with and/or understanding-what.

8 Epilogue

The literature on idealization in physics touches on virtually every major topic in the philosophy of science, so we have covered only the tip of the iceberg. In this Element, I stressed how there are numerous characterizations of idealizations, various reasons to idealize, and many roles played by idealization. I noted the need to attend to an epistemic-logical justificatory problem, the role played by both in-principle de-idealization (broadly construed) and the in-principle/in-practice distinction in solving said problem, and the difficulties associated with providing such justification. Such difficulties also extend to providing an adequate taxonomy of idealization and to some degree stem from the fact that the nature of idealization is entangled with commitments to epistemic and ontological views of science and the world, including issues such as interpretation of background theories, modality, scale and levels, fundamentality, as well as induction and confirmation. If indeed the justificatory problem can be solved while maintaining the indispensability of idealizations, and a paradox in the way of imputing contradictory properties to target systems can be avoided, then I have suggested that realists may need to commit to stronger views than they intended, or else embrace acceptable anti-realist positions. I have also suggested (particularly in the case of the AB effect) that idealizations play a role in understanding-what some phenomena are in the first place and in understanding the structure of theory in light of said phenomena.

References

Aharonov, Y., & D. Bohm. 1959. "Significance of Electromagnetic Potentials in the Quantum Theory." *Physical Review*, 115: 485–491.

Ardourel, V. 2018. "The Infinite Limit As an Eliminable Approximation for Phase Transitions." *Studies in History and Philosophy of Modern Physics*, 62: 71–84.

Ardourel, V., & J. Jebeile. 2017. "On the Presumed Superiority of Analytical Solutions over Numerical Methods." *European Journal for Philosophy of Science*, 7: 201–220.

Arovas, D. P., J. R. Schrieffer, & F. Wilczek. 1984. "Fractional Statistics and the Quantum Hall Effect." *Physical Review Letters*, 53: 722–723.

Bacciagaluppi, G. 2020. "The Role of Decoherence in Quantum Mechanics." *Stanford Encyclopedia of Philosophy* (Fall 2020 Edition), Edward N. Zalta (ed.). https://plato.stanford.edu/archives/fall2020/entries/qm-decoherence.

Bain, J. 2013. "Emergence in Effective Field Theories." *European Journal for Philosophy of Science*, 3: 257–273.

Bain, J. 2016. "Emergence and Mechanism in the Fractional Quantum Hall Effect." *Studies in History and Philosophy of Modern Physics*, 56: 27–38.

Baker, A. 2005. "Are There Genuine Mathematical Explanations of Physical Phenomena?" *Mind*, 114: 223–238.

Baker, A. 2009. "Mathematical Explanation in Science." *British Journal for the Philosophy of Science*, 60: 611–633.

Ballesteros, M., & R. Weder. 2009. "The Aharonov–Bohm Effect and Tonomura et al. Experiments: Rigorous Results." *Journal of Mathematical Physics*, 50: 122108.

Ballesteros, M., & R. Weder. 2011. "Aharonov–Bohm Effect and High-Velocity Estimates of Solutions to the Schrödinger Equation." *Communications in Mathematical Physics*, 303(1): 175–211.

Bangu, S. 2019. "Discontinuities and Singularities, Data and Phenomena: For Referentialism." *Synthese*, 196: 1919–1937.

Baron, S. 2016. "The Explanatory Dispensability of Idealizations." *Synthese*, 193: 365–386.

Baron, S. 2019. "Infinite Lies and Explanatory Ties: Idealization in Phase Transitions." *Synthese*, 196: 1939–1961.

Bartha, P. 2019. "Analogy and Analogical Reasoning." *Stanford Encyclopedia of Philosophy* (Spring 2019 Edition), Edward N. Zalta (ed.). https://plato.stanford.edu/archives/spr2019/entries/reasoning-analogy.

Batterman, R. 2002. *The Devil in the Details: Asymptotic Reasoning in Explanation, Reduction, and Emergence*. New York: Oxford University Press.

Batterman, R. 2006. "Hydrodynamics versus Molecular dynamics: Intertheory relations in condensed matter physics. Philosophy of Science, 73(5), 888–904.

Batterman, R. 2021. *A Middle Way: A Non-fundamental Approach to Many-Body Physics*. Oxford: Oxford University Press.

Batterman, R., & C. Rice. 2014. "Minimal Model Explanations." *Philosophy of Science*, 81(3): 349–376.

Baumberger, C. 2011. "Types of Understanding: Their Nature and Their Relation to Knowledge." *Conceptus*, 40: 67–88.

Bocchieri, P., & A. Loinger. 1978. "Nonexistence of the Aharonov–Bohm Effect." *Nuovo Cimento*, 47A: 475–482.

Bocchieri, P., & A. Loinger. 1981. "Charges in Multiply Connected Spaces." *Nuovo Cimento*, 66: 164–172.

Bokulich, A. 2008. *Reexamining the Quantum-Classical Relation: Beyond Reductionism and Pluralism*. Cambridge: Cambridge University Press.

Borwein, J., & R. Crandall. 2013. "Closed Forms: What They Are and Why We Care." *Notices of the American Mathematical Society*, 60(1): 50–65.

Boyer, T. H. 2000. "Does the Aharonov–Bohm Effect Exist?" *Foundations of Physics*, 30(6): 893–905.

Bueno, O., & S. French. 2018. *Applying Mathematics: Immersion, Inference, Interpretation*. Oxford: Oxford University Press.

Butterfield, J. 2011. "Less Is Different: Emergence and Reduction Reconciled." *Foundations of Physics*, 41(6): 1065–1135.

Cartwright, N. 1983. *How the Laws of Physics Lie*. New York: Clarendon.

Chakravartty, A. 2017. "Scientific Realism." *Stanford Encyclopedia of Philosophy* (Summer 2017 Edition), Edward N. Zalta (ed.). https://plato.stanford.edu/archives/sum2017/entries/scientific-realism.

Chalmers, D. J. 2006. "Strong and Weak Emergences." In P. Clayton & P. Davies (eds.), *The Re-emergence of Emergence: The Emergentist Hypothesis from Science to Religion* (pp. 244–257). Oxford: Oxford University Press.

Chambers, R. G. 1960. "Shift of an Electron Interference Pattern by Enclosed Magnetic Flux." *Physical Review Letters*, 5(1): 3–5.

Cheng, T.-P. 2013. *Einstein's Physics: Atoms, Quanta, and Relativity Derived, Explained, and Appraised*. Oxford: Oxford University Press.

Colyvan, M. (2001). *The indispensability of mathematics*. New York: Oxford University Press.

Crease, R. P. 2002. "The Most Beautiful Experiment." *Physics World*, 15(9): 19–20.

Darrigol, O. 2013. "For a Philosophy of Hydrodynamics." In R. Batterman (ed.), *The Oxford Handbook of Philosophy of Physics* (pp. 224–254). Oxford: Oxford University Press.

Davey, K. 2011. "Idealizations and Contextualism in Physics." *Philosophy of Science*, 78: 16–38.

de Bianchi, S. 2016. "Which Explanatory Role for Mathematics in Scientific Models? Reply to 'The Explanatory Dispensability of Idealizations.'" *Synthese*, 193: 387–401. https://doi.org/10.1007/s11229-015-0795-0.

de Oliveira, C. R., & M. Pereira. 2008. "Mathematical Justification of the Aharonov–Bohm Hamiltonian." *Journal of Statistical Physics*, 133: 1175–1184.

de Oliveira, C. R., & M. Pereira. 2010. "Scattering and Self-Adjoint Extensions of the Aharonov–Bohm Hamiltonian." *Journal of Physics A: Mathematical and Theoretical*, 43: 1–29.

de Oliveira, C. R., & M. Pereira. 2011. "Impenetrability of Aharonov–Bohm Solenoids: Proof of Norm Resolvent Convergence." *Letters in Mathematical Physics*, 95: 41–51.

de Regt, H. W. 2017. *Understanding Scientific Understanding*. Oxford: Oxford University Press.

Diacu, F. 1996. "The Solution of the N-body Problem." *Mathematical Intelligencer*, 18(3): 66–70.

Dougherty, J. 2021. "The Non-ideal Theory of the Aharonov–Bohm Effect." *Synthese*, 198:12195–12221. https://doi.org/10.1007/s11229-020-02859-x.

Doyle, Y., E. Spencer, G. Noah, & K. Khalifa. 2019. "Non-factive Understanding: A Statement and Defense." *Journal for General Philosophy of Science*, 50: 345–365.

Earman, J. 2004. "Curie's Principle and Spontaneous Symmetry Breaking." *International Studies in the Philosophy of Science*, 18(2–3): 173–198.

Earman, J. 2019. "The Role of Idealization in the Aharonov–Bohm Effect." *Synthese*, 196: 1991–2019.

Einstein, A. 1926/1956. *Investigations on the Theory of Brownian Movement*. R. Fürth & A. D. Cowper (eds.). Mineola, NY: Dover.

Elgin, C. 2017. "Exemplification in Understanding." In S. R. Grimm, C. Baumberger, & S. Ammon (eds.), *Explaining Understanding: New Perspectives from Epistemology and Philosophy of Science* (pp. 76–92). New York: Routledge.

Elgin, M., & E. Sober. 2002. "Cartwright on Explanation and Idealization." *Erkentniss*, 57: 441–450.

Elliott-Graves, A., & M. Weisberg. 2014. "Idealization." *Philosophy Compass* 9(3): 176–185.

Ellis, B. 1992. "Idealization in Science." In C. Dilworth (ed.), *Idealization IV: Intelligibility in Science* (pp. 265–282). Amsterdam: Rodopi.

Ellis, G. F. 2020. "Emergence in Solid State Physics and Biology." *Foundations of Physics*, 50(10): 1098–1139.

Fletcher, S., P. Palacios, L. Ruetsche, & E. Shech. 2019a. "Infinite Idealizations in Science: An Introduction." *Synthese*, 196: 1657–1669.

Fletcher, S., P. Palacios, L. Ruetsche, & E. Shech. 2019b. *Infinite Idealization in Science*. Special issue of *Synthese*, 196(5).

French., S. 2020. *There Are No Such Things As Theories*. Oxford: Oxford University Press.

Frigg, R. 2008. "A Field Guide to Recent Work on the Foundations of Statistical Mechanics." In Dean Rickles (ed.), *Ashgate Companion to Contemporary Philosophy of Physics* (pp. 99–196). London: Ashgate.

Frigg, R., & S. Hartmann. 2020. "Models in Science." *Stanford Encyclopedia of Philosophy* (Spring 2020 Edition), Edward N. Zalta (ed.). https://plato .stanford.edu/archives/spr2020/entries/models-science.

Frigg, R., & J. Nguyen. 2020. "Scientific Representation." *Stanford Encyclopedia of Philosophy* (Spring 2020 Edition), Edward N. Zalta (ed.). https://plato.stanford.edu/archives/spr2020/entries/scientific-representation.

Gelfert, A. 2016. *How to Do Science with Models: A Philosophical Primer*. Cham: Springer.

Georgi, H. 1993. "Effective Field Theory." *Annual Review of Nuclear and Particle Science*, 43(1): 209–252.

Gillett, C. 2016. *Reduction and Emergence in Science and Philosophy*. Cambridge: Cambridge University Press.

Godfrey-Smith, P. 2009. "Abstractions, Idealizations and Evolutionary Biology." In *Mapping the Future of Biology*. Boston Studies in the Philosophy of Science, Vol. 266 (pp. 47–56). Cham: Springer.

Goldstein, H., C. Poole, & J. Safko. 2002. *Classical Mechanics*. Third Edition. Addison Wesley.

Gryb, S., P. Palacios, & K. P. Thébault. 2021. "On the Universality of Hawking Radiation." *British Journal for the Philosophy of Science*, 72(3): 809–837.

Guggenheim, E. A. 1945. "The Principle of Corresponding States." *Journal of Chemical Physics*, 13(7): 253–261.

Harte, J. (1988) *Consider A Spherical Cow: A Course in Environmental Problem Solving*. Sausalito, CA: University Science Books

Healey, R. 1997. "Nonlocality and the Aharonov–Bohm Effect." *Philosophy of Science*, 64: 18–41.

Healey, R. 1999. "Quantum Analogies: A Reply to Maudlin." *Philosophy of Science*, 66: 440–447.

Hempel, C. G., & P. Oppenheim. 1948 [1965]. "Studies in the Logic of Explanation." *Philosophy of Science*, 15(2): 135–175. Reprinted in Hempel, C. G. 1965. *Aspects of Scientific Explanation and Other Essays in the Philosophy of Science* (pp. 245–290). New York: Free Press.

Hilpinen, R. 1976. "Approximate Truth and Truthlikeness." In M. Przełecki, K. Szaniawski, R.Wójcicki, & G. Malinowski (eds.), *Formal Methods in the Methodology of Empirical Sciences* (pp. 19–42). Dordrecht: Springer.

Homes, T. 2022. "Reckoning with Continuum Idealizations: Some Lessons from Soil Hydrology." *Philosophy of Science*, 89: 319–336.

Huggett, N., & R. Weingard. 1995. "The Renormalization Group and Effective Field Theories." *Synthese*, 102(1): 171–194.

Humphreys, P. 2004. *Extending Ourselves: Computational Science, Empiricism, and Scientific Method*. Oxford: Oxford University Press.

Hüttemann, A. 2002. "Idealizations in Physics." In M. Ferrari & I.-O. Stamatescu (eds.), *Symbolic and Physical Knowledge: On the Conceptual Structure of Physics* (pp. 177–192). Berlin: Springer.

Jansson, L. Forthcoming. *Explanation in Physics*. Cambridge University Press.

Jacquart, M. Forthcoming. *Models in Physics*. Cambridge University Press.

Jacquart, M., E. Shech, & M. Zach. 2022. *Representation, Idealization, and Explanation in Science*. Special Issue of *Studies in History and Philosophy of Science*. https://doi.org/10.1016/j.shpsa.2022.09.003.

Jones, M. R. 2005. "Idealization and Abstraction: A Framework." In M. Jones & N. Cartwright (eds.), *Idealizations XII: Correcting the Model. Idealizations and Abstraction in the Sciences* (pp. 173–217). Amsterdam: Rodopi.

Jones, N. 2006. "Ineliminable Idealizations, Phase Transitions and Irreversibility." PhD diss. Ohio State University.

Ladyman, J. 2008. "Idealization." In S. Psillos & M. Curd (eds.), *The Routledge Companion to Philosophy of Science* (pp. 358–366). London: Routledge Taylor & Francis Group.

Ladyman, J. 2018. "Scientific Realism Again." *Spontaneous Generations: A Journal for the History and Philosophy of Science*, 9(1): 99–107.

Ladyman, J., & D. Ross. 2007. *Every Thing Must Go: Metaphysics Naturalised*. Oxford: Oxford University Press.

Ladyman, J., & K. Wiesner. 2020. *What Is a Complex System?* New Haven, CT: Yale University Press.

Landsman, N. P. 2016. "Quantization and Superselection Sectors III: Multiply Connected Spaces and Indistinguishable Particles." *Reviews in Mathematical Physics*, 28: 1650019.

Le Bihan, S. 2017. "Enlightening Falsehoods: A Modal View of Scientific Understanding." In S. R. Grimm, C. Baumberger, & S. Ammon (eds.), *Explaining Understanding: New Perspectives from Epistemology and Philosophy of Science* (pp. 111–136). New York: Routledge.

Leggett, A. J. 1992. "On the Nature of Research in Condensed-State Physics." *Foundations of Physics*, 22(2): 221–233.

Leng, M. 2012. "Taking It Easy: A Response to Colyvan." *Mind*, 121: 983–996.

Levins, R. 1966. "The Strategy of Model Building in Population Biology." In E. Sober (ed.), *Conceptual Issues in Evolutionary Biology*. First Edition (pp. 18–27). Cambridge, MA: MIT Press.

Levy, A. 2015. "Modeling without Models." *Philosophical Studies*, 172(3): 781–798.

Levy, A. 2018. "Idealization and Abstraction: Refining the Distinction." *Synthese*, 1–18.

Levy, A. 2020. "Metaphor and Scientific Explanation." In P. Godfrey-Smith & A. Levy (eds.), *The Scientific Imagination* (pp. 280–303). Oxford: Oxford University Press.

Liu, C. 2004. "Laws and Models in a Theory of Idealization." *Synthese*, 138: 363–385.

Liu, C. 2019. "Infinite Idealization and Contextual Realism." *Synthese*, 196: 1885–1918.

Luu, T., & U.-G. Meißner. 2019. "On the Topic of Emergence from an Effective Field Theory Perspective." arXiv preprint arXiv:1910.13770.

Kadanoff, L. P. 2000. *Statistical Physics: Statics, Dynamics and Renormalization*. Singapore: World Scientific.

Kelp, C. 2015. "Understanding Phenomena." *Synthese*, 192 (12): 3799–3816.

Khalifa, K. 2017. *Understanding, Explanation, and Scientific Knowledge*. Cambridge: Cambridge University Press.

Klitzing, K. V., G. Dorda, & M. Pepper. 1980. "New Method for High-Accuracy Determination of the Fine-Structure Constant Based on Quantized Hall Resistance." *Physical Review Letters*, 45: 494–497.

Magni, C., & F. Valz-Gris. 1995. "Can Elementary Quantum Mechanics Explain the Aharonov–Bohm Effect?" *Journal of Mathematical Physics*, 36(1): 177–186.

Mäki, U. 1994. "Isolation, Idealization and Truth in Economics." In B. Hamminga & N. B. de Marchi (eds.), *Idealization VI: Idealization in Economics*. Poznan Studies in the Philosophy of the Sciences and the Humanities, Vol. 38 (pp. 147–168). Amsterdam: Rodopi.

Maudlin, T. 1998. "Healey on the Aharonov–Bohm Effect." *Philosophy of Science*, 65: 361–368.

Maynard Smith, J., & G. R. Price. 1973. "The Logic of Animal Conflict." *Nature*, 246: 15–18.

McMullin, E. 1985. "Galilean Idealization." *Studies in the History and Philosophy of Science*, 16: 247–73.

Menon, T., & C. Callender. 2013. "Turn and Face the Strange . . . Ch-ch-changes: Philosophical Questions Raised by Phase Transitions." In R. W. Batterman (ed.), *The Oxford Handbook of Philosophy of Physics* (pp. 189–223). Oxford: Oxford University Press.

Messiah, A. M. 1962. *Quantum Mechanics*. New York: Wiley.

Möllenstedt, G., & W. Bayh. 1962. "Kontinuierliche Phasenschiebung von Elektronenwellen im kraftfeldfreien Raum durch das magnetische Vektorpotential eines Solenoids." *Zeitschrift für Physik*, 169: 299–305.

Morrison, M. 2012. "Emergent Physics and Micro-ontology." *Philosophy of Science*, 79: 141–166.

Morrison, M. 2015. *Reconstructing Reality: Models, Mathematics, and Simulations*. Oxford: Oxford University Press.

Musgrave, A. 1981. "'Unreal Assumptions' in Economic Theory: The F-Twist Untwisted." *Kyklos*, 34: 377–387.

Musielak, Z. E., & E. Quarles. 2014. "The Three-Body Problem." *Reports on Progress in Physics*, 77: 065901.

Newman, M. P. 2017. "Theoretical Understanding in Science." *British Journal for the Philosophy of Science*, 68(2): 571–595.

Norton, J. D. 2008. "The Dome: An Unexpectedly Simple Failure of Determinism." *Philosophy of Science*, 75: 786–798.

Norton, J. D. 2012. "Approximations and Idealizations: Why the Difference Matters." *Philosophy of Science*, 79: 207–232.

Norton, J. D. 2016. "The Impossible Process: Thermodynamic Reversibility." *Studies in History and Philosophy of Science B*, 55: 43–61.

Nowak, L. 2000. "The Idealizational Approach to Science: A New Survey." In I. Nowakowa & L. Nowak (eds.), *Idealization X: The Richness of Idealization* (pp. 109–185). Amsterdam: Rodopi.

Oddie, G. 2016. "Truthlikeness." *Stanford Encyclopedia of Philosophy* (Winter 2016 Edition), Edward N. Zalta (ed.). https://plato.stanford.edu/archives/win2016/entries/truthlikeness.

Olariu, S., & I. Popescu. 1985. "The Quantum Effects of Electromagnetic Fluxes." *Reviews of Modern Physics*, 57(2): 339e449.

Palacios, P. 2019. "Phase Transitions: A Challenge for Intertheoretic Reduction?" *Philosophy of Science*, 86(4): 612–640.

Palacios, P. 2022. *Emergence and Reduction in Physics*. Cambridge: Cambridge University Press.

Palacios, P., & G. Valente. 2021. "The Paradox of Infinite Limits: A Realist Response." In T. Lyons & P. Vickers (eds.), *Contemporary Scientific Realism* (pp. 312–349). Oxford: Oxford University Press.

Pincock, C. 2012. *Mathematics and Scientific Representation*. Oxford: Oxford University Press.

Pincock, C. 2020. "Concrete Scale Models, Essential Idealization, and Causal Explanation." *British Journal for Philosophy of Science*, 73(2): 1–20.

Portides, D. 2018. "Idealization and Abstraction in Scientific Modeling." *Synthese*, 1–23.

Potochnik, A. 2017. *Idealization and the Aim of Science*. Chicago, IL: University of Chicago University Press.

Psillos, S. 2011. "Living with the Abstract: Realism and Models." *Synthese*, 180: 3–17.

Putnam, H. 1971. *Philosophy of Logic*. New York: Harper.

Quine, W. V. O. 1981. *Theories and Things*. Cambridge, MA: Harvard University Press.

Reed, M., & B. Simon. 1980. *Methods of Modern Mathematical Physics* (Vols. 1–4). San Diego: Academic Press.

Rice, C. 2021. *Leveraging Distortions: Explanation, Idealizations, and Universality in Science*. Cambridge, MA: MIT Press.

Ridderbos, T. M., & M. L. G. Redhead. 1998. "The Spin-Echo Experiments and the Second Law of Thermodynamics." *Foundations of Physics*, 28: 1237–1270.

Rohwer, Y., & C. Rice. 2013. "Hypothetical Pattern Idealization and Explanatory Models." *Philosophy of Science*, 80: 334–355.

Ruelle, D. 2004. *Thermodynamic Formalism*. Second Edition. Cambridge: Cambridge University Press.

Ruetsche, L. 2011. *Interpreting Quantum Theories: The Art of the Possible*. Oxford: Oxford University Press.

Saatsi, J. 2016. "Models, Idealisations, and Realism." In E. Ippoliti, F. Sterpetti, & T. Nickles (eds.), *Models and Inferences in Science* (pp. 173–189). Cham: Springer.

Schelling, T. 1978. *Micromotives and Macrobehavior*. New York: Norton.

Shaffer, M. J. 2012. *Counterfactuals and Scientific Realism*. Basingstoke: Palgrave MacMillan.

Shech, E. 2013. "What Is the 'Paradox of Phase Transitions?'" *Philosophy of Science*, 80: 1170–1181.

Shech, E. 2015a. "Scientific Misrepresentation and Guides to Ontology: The Need for Representational Code and Contents." *Synthese*, 192(11): 3463–3485.

Shech, E. 2015b. "Two Approaches to Fractional Statistics in the Quantum Hall Effect: Idealizations and the Curious Case of the Anyon." *Foundations of Physics*, 45(9): 1063–1110.

Shech, E. 2016. "Fiction, Depiction, and the Complementarity Thesis in Art and Science." *The Monist*, 99(3): 311–332.

Shech, E. 2018a. "Infinite Idealizations in Physics." *Philosophy Compass*, 13(9): e12514.

Shech, E. 2018b. "Idealizations, Essential Self-Adjointness, and Minimal Model Explanation in the Aharonov-Bohm Effect." *Synthese*, 195: 4839–4863.

Shech, E. 2019a. "Philosophical Issues Concerning Phase Transitions and Anyons: Emergence, Reduction, and Explanatory Fictions." *Erkenntnis* 84(3): 585–615.

Shech, E. 2019b. "Infinitesimal Idealization, Easy Road Nominalism, and Fractional Quantum Statistics." *Synthese*, 156(5): 1963–1990.

Shech, E. 2019c. "Historical Inductions Meet the Material Theory." *Philosophy of Science*, 86(5): 918–929.

Shech, E. 2022a. "Scientific Understanding in the Aharonov–Bohm Effect." *Theoria*. https://doi.org/10.1111/theo.12409.

Shech, E. 2022b. "Darwinian-Selectionist Explanation, Radical Theory Change, and the Observable-Unobservable Dichotomy." *International Studies in Philosophy of Science*. https://doi.org/10.1080/02698595.2022.2092824.

Shech, E., & A. Gelfert. 2019. "The Exploratory Role of Models and Idealizations." Studia Metodologiczne – Dissertationes Methodologicae. ISSN 0039-324X Issue on Culture(s) of Modelling in Science(s) (39).

Shech, E., & P. McGivern. 2021. "Fundamentality, Scale, and the Fractional Quantum Hall Effect." *Erkenntnis*, 86: 1411–1430.

Shech, E., M. Zach, & M. Jacquart. 2022. *Idealization, Representation, and Explanation across the Sciences*. Special issues in *Studies in History & Philosophy of Science*. www.sciencedirect.com/journal/studies-in-history-and-philosophy-of-science/special-issue/10X9K0G3H30.

Sklar, L. 2000. *Theory and Truth: Philosophical Critique within Foundational Science*. Oxford: Oxford University Press.

Stanley, H. E. 1971. *Introduction to Phase Transitions and Critical Phenomena*. New York: Oxford University Press.

Stern, A. 2008. "Anyons and the Quantum Hall Effect: A Pedagogical Review." *Annalen der Physik*, 323: 204–249.

Stone, N. C., & N. W. C. Leigh. 2019. "A Statistical Solution to the Chaotic, Non-hierarchical Three-Body Problem." *Nature*, 576(19/26): 406–410.

Strevens, M. 2008. *Depth: An Account of Scientific Explanation*. Cambridge, MA: Harvard University Press.

Strevens, M. 2013. "No Understanding without Explanation." *Studies in History and Philosophy of Science*, 44: 510–515.

Strevens, M. 2017. "How Idealizations Provide Understanding." In S. R. Grimm, C. Baumberger, & S. Ammon (eds.), *Explaining Understanding: New Perspectives from Epistemology and Philosophy of Science* (pp. 37–49). New York: Routledge.

Strocchi, F., & A. S. Wightman. 1974. Proof of the Charge Superselection Rule in Local Relativistic Quantum Field Theory. *Journal of Mathematical Physics*, 15: 2189–2224.

Stuart, M. T. 2018. "How Thought Experiments Increase Understanding." in M. T. Stuart, Y. J. H. Fehige, & J. R. Brown (eds.), *The Routledge Companion to Thought Experiments* (pp. 526–544). London: Routledge.

Sullivan, E., & K. Khalifa. 2019. "Idealizations and Understanding: Much Ado about Nothing?" *Australasian Journal of Philosophy*, 97(4): 673–689.

Sundman, K. 1912. "Mèmoire sur le problème des trois corps." *Acta Mathematica*, 36: 105–179.

Swoyer, C. 1991. "Structural Representation and Surrogative Reasoning." *Synthese*, 87: 449–508.

Toon, A. 2012. *Models As Make-Believe: Imagination, Fiction and Scientific Representation*. Basingstoke: Palgrave Macmillan.

Tonomura, A. 1999. *Electron Holography*. Berlin: Springer.

Tonomura, A., Osakabe, N., Tsuyoshi, M. et al. 1986. "Evidence for Aharonov–Bohm Effect with Magnetic Field Completely Shielded from Electron Wave." *Physical Review Letter* 56: 792–795.

Tsui, D. C., H. L. Stormer, & A. C. Gossard. 1982. "Two-Dimensional Magnetotransport in the Extreme Quantum Limit." *Physical Review Letters*, 48(22): 1559–1562.

Valente, G. 2019. "On the Paradox of Reversible Processes in Thermodynamics." *Synthese*, 196: 1761–1781.

Valtonen, M., & H. Karttunun. 2005. *The Three-Body Problem*. Cambridge: Cambridge University Press.

Wang, Q.-D. 1991. "The Global Solution of the n-Body Problem." *Celestial Mechanics and Dynamics Astronomy*, 50: 73–88.

Weisberg, M. 2013. *Simulation and Similarity: Using Models to Understand the World*. Oxford: Oxford University Press.

Wilson, M. 2013. "What Is 'Classical Mechanics' Anyway?" In Robert Batterman (ed.), *The Oxford Handbook of Philosophy of Physics* (pp. 224–254). Oxford: Oxford University Press.

Winsberg, E. 2010. *Science in the Age of Computer Simulation*. Chicago, IL: University of Chicago Press.

Woodward, J. 2003. *Making Things Happen: A Theory of Causal Explanation*. Oxford: Oxford University Press.

Wu, J. 2021. "Explaining Universality: Infinite Limit Systems in the Renormalization Group Method." *Synthese*, 199: 14897–14930.

Acknowledgments

Thanks to the editor, James Weatherall, and to Auburn University's Department of Philosophy and chair, Michael Watkins, for their support. Thank you also to two anonymous reviewers and especially to Michel Smith for comments and suggestions. Additionally, thank you to John Wiley and Sons and Springer Nature for letting me use bits and pieces of my Shech (2019a, 2019b, 2022a). I'm very grateful to John Earman, John Norton, Robert Batterman, and Laura Ruetsche for their feedback on my work throughout the years, much of which was the basis for this Element. Most important, thank you to my parents, Orit and Aharon Shech, my sisters, Naharin and Nadine Shech, and my wife, Isabel Shech, for their unwavering support and boundless love – I dedicate this Element to them.

Cambridge Elements ☰

The Philosophy of Physics

James Owen Weatherall
University of California, Irvine

James Owen Weatherall is Professor of Logic and Philosophy of Science at the University of California, Irvine. He is the author, with Cailin O'Connor, of *The Misinformation Age: How False Beliefs Spread* (Yale, 2019), which was selected as a *New York Times* Editors' Choice and Recommended Reading by *Scientific American*. His previous books were *Void: The Strange Physics of Nothing* (Yale, 2016) and the *New York Times* bestseller *The Physics of Wall Street: A Brief History of Predicting the Unpredictable* (Houghton Mifflin Harcourt, 2013). He has published approximately fifty peer-reviewed research articles in journals in leading physics and philosophy of science journals and has delivered over 100 invited academic talks and public lectures.

About the Series

This Cambridge Elements series provides concise and structured introductions to all the central topics in the philosophy of physics. The Elements in the series are written by distinguished senior scholars and bright junior scholars with relevant expertise, producing balanced, comprehensive coverage of multiple perspectives in the philosophy of physics.

Cambridge Elements $^{\equiv}$

The Philosophy of Physics

Printed in the United States
by Baker & Taylor Publisher Services